# Dialogues With A Shaman Teacher

## Into the Silence

## Winged Wolf

Higher Consciousness Books
1996

Cover Portait by Marita Smith and Alaya Hughes taken at the 1995 Gathering of the Eagle Tribe/ The Shamanic Path of Soul™.

---

Winged Wolf, Soul Vision, The Eagle Tribe, The Path of Soul, The Shamanic Path of Soul, Companion Energy, and The Tribe of Eagles are registered trade marks/trade names.

---

Higher Consciousness Books
Division of Coastline Publishing Company
Post Office Box 268
Deer Harbor, Washington  98243
Phone/Fax (360) 376-3700


Printed in the United States of America


Library of Congress Catalog No.: 96-084982
ISBN: 0-932927-12-2

Leaping Deer

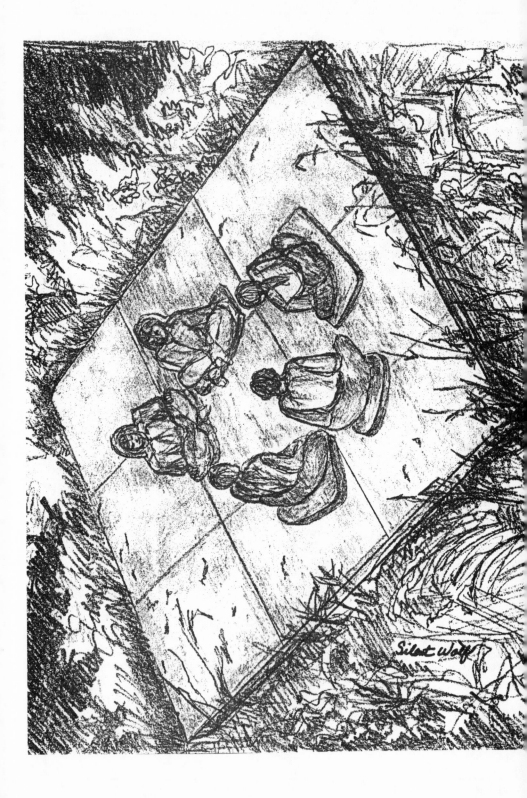

**With gratitude to all my apprentices for their impeccability and wholeheartedness in making this book possible.**

... a special 'thank you' to Easy Walker, who lovingly typeset the text and coordinated the energy of typists, proofreaders, editors, and artists.

Silent Wolf...Wings of Change..
Standing Turtle.. Many Visions...
Free to Fly.

# TABLE OF CONTENTS

# PREFACE

It is said that when the student is ready, the teacher appears. You can look and look for a Shaman teacher and never find one, but a Shaman teacher will find you. Perhaps your teacher may have a striking influence on you while you are reading a book like this one. Maybe you discovered the book in an odd way; possibly it fell off a library shelf to your feet. Or when you first meet, you may have a striking familiarity or a feeling of connection to the Shaman who will teach you; you will simply know. A Shaman teacher has an incredible presence, a powerful life force and clarity of mind. You may feel this person knows everything about you even though you have just met.

It is truly an honor to write the foreword for *Dialogues with A Shaman Teacher*. We see this book as the ultimate book to have at your bedside, to open at random and read for immediate inspiration. The more each dialogue is read, the deeper the understanding becomes. This is because each time a dialogue is reread, the reader reads if from a different state of consciousness, received on many subconscious levels and inner dimensions depending upon the readers' willingness to expand their consciousness.

The teachings as written, are literal and based on universal truth and natural laws.

The Shamanic Path of Soul is a process of living one's own knowledge as Soul, becoming one with that witness and observer part of each of us. How to live as Soul experientially is clearly outlined in this book.

Dialogues are recorded between Shaman Teacher and her apprentices 'Between the Wind'. Each morning,

Winged Wolf begins the day speaking to her apprentices on subjects that are totally appropriate to the moment, for the particular growth and spiritual advancement of the apprentices present.

As you, the reader, begin your own journey through the dialogues, you will see just how the subjects presented themselves and evolved. You will feel the power and inspiration that Winged Wolf's apprentices experienced by being in a Shaman's presence. The energy imparted by Winged Wolf, whose life is an example of the higher teachings and who lives impeccably in the moment, is empowering beyond the words spoken.

Many books have been written on the subject of attaining enlightenment and on apprenticing with a Shaman teacher, but *Dialogues with a Shaman Teacher* is unique in that it is a writing of teachings that originate in the present moment as they are manifested. As she delivers charged words to apprentices in her presence, all other apprentices benefit as they hear those words, or rather feel their energy, on some other level, depending on their degree of awareness. And, beyond apprentices, all readers will, in turn, benefit. It is the rippling effect moving outward, uplifting all levels of consciousness.

This is a teacher who lives her impeccability for all to see. Her life is her teaching.

There was basically no editing involved in the recording of these dialogues. They are written as they occurred. There was an attempt to insure that the spoken word translated into a comfortable flow for the reader to follow.

We hope you, the reader, find these dialogues as enlightening and enlivening.


*Wings of Change and Silent Wolf*

# The Shamanic Path of Soul

Dear Reader:

Shamanism, as it referred to in this book, is defined as a science of living life splendidly - abundantly and joyfully - in harmony with the environment and all its creatures. The science of Shamanism dictates that the environment produces a mirror image of one's every thought and one's every action, thus setting up a cycle for each mental image passing through one's mind. The more strongly the mental image is felt, the more complex and dramatic the reflection is enacted in one's personal life. In other words, images passing through your mind are the "stuff" that makes up your life. Such is the nature of personal responsibility.

Shamanism also means the *impeccable* way, of aligning your actions with your dreams, or doing what you *dream* to do. By living as you want, you live honestly, bypassing drudgery, to become a genuinely happy and fulfilled human being. This is the state of consciousness that enables one to become capable of *service* to mankind. When you live impeccably to yourself, you live impeccably to all - husband, wife, mother, father, child, and in your professions, as well.

Out of impeccability, an individual learns wholeheartedness, giving totally of theirself to the *present moment*, to whatever it is you are doing. Wholeheartedness develops a great passion and zest for life, a willingness, eagerness without expectation, to participate in the even flow of universal giving and receiving.

And out of wholeheartedness develops divine love, which is compassion for all sentient and non-sentient beings. Divine love produces an awareness of the Oneness of all life, of recognizing that the individual giving the attention and the object of the attention are One and the same. Herein you come upon the recognition that life is a dream and that you are the dreamer, and, suddenly, you realize the true nature of yourself as Soul.

As Soul, you realize the nature of the Void or God and yourself as a part of *That*. And here we come to name this path - The Shamanic Path of Soul™

It is a pure teaching, as clean as the teacher dares it to be. The teacher walks ahead, into the depth of the Void to lead the way as an embodiment of the Godhead.

I did not originate The Shamanic Path of Soul. My teachers of this lifetime redirected me there. My most recent teacher, Alana Spirit Changer, was a Sioux Native American Shaman/Medicine Woman. My apprenticeship is storied in my books *Woman Between the Wind, The Flight of Winged Wolf, Circle of Power,* and concludes with her translation in *The Shamanic Journey of Living as Soul*. She is carried in my heart with gratitude for teaching me to *walk my talk*. The other major teacher in my life was a Tibetan who visited me in my childhood to encourage me to walk beyond my fears. He introduced me to the teaching of the Tibetan Saint Milarepa, and taught me to center myself at the Third Eye; and, then, one day disappeared out of my life, until many years later. This Tibetan teacher, who I will call X, is a living human being. His Shaman Consciousness makes him omnipresent and, because of the work I am dedicated to do, his presence is now often at my side. Alana Spirit Changer knew him; although, except to acknowledge his presence, never spoke of him to me.

It is interesting to note that there is a close relationship between the teachings of Tibetan Shamanism

11

and Native American Shamanism. There is almost no difference, except as displayed in rituals, customs and traditions. Since I am an American, with no Native American or Tibetan roots in this lifetime, I do not teach their rituals, customs, nor traditions. I teach, using our contemporary lifestyles as ritual, and the customs, and the traditions of our Western countries as our ceremony for perfecting life. This is accomplished by empowering you to see through the illusion.

Welcome to the Shamanic Path of Soul.

As Soul -

Winged Wolf

# BEYOND DUALITIES

**Winged Wolf:** "The topic for this evening is 'Beyond Dualities'. This is a fitting title because today we had light and warmth, tonight we are having darkness and chill. So, you see, there are opposites, like two sides of a coin - heads and tails. We have this side of the mountain and the other side of the mountain. Life seems to be established on duality.

"Spiritually, however, there is a place beyond dualities. There still exists a front and a back to things, but the front and the back are not separated. They become one with the whole of what you are looking at. The front and the back of the mountain are still the mountain. It is not the front or the back of the mountain, it is the mountain itself.

"If you were to go down to the lake and dip your hand into the water, you would pull up many droplets. Each droplet is a part of the lake. It is still the whole. There is this side and that side. There is the top of the lake and the bottom of the lake. It is still the lake.

"When we view difficulties in life, we study different sides of a situation. There is this side and there is that side; so, dualities in life seem to come in many packages.

"We are not concerned with compartmentalizing life as Soul. As Soul, there is only One. One everything! That does not mean that both sides aren't seen. They are seen as varying energy. It is the energy of each that is perceived.

"In other words, when you look at something, you perceive the energy of it, rather than inspecting this side versus that side. When you compare this side to that side, there is the danger of getting hooked into observing differences, instead of seeing the whole, where you

13

become aware of both sides and view each as an energy of the whole.

"When one is coming from a mental viewpoint, they look at one side versus the other side and they compare. As Soul, since there are no dualities, there is no comparison. You see life as a whole. As a whole, one thing equals another. You and I may be individuals, but you and I are both Soul. It is not your Soul, or my Soul. It is Soul! So you see, as Soul, we are really ONE.

"As Soul, we live beyond dualities. This does not mean that one gives up their individual reality. We are here in this world to experience life so we develop a personality and develop viewpoints to do this. One person becomes a doctor; another a lawyer; another a merchant; another a teacher; another delivers newspapers. Do you see? These are expressions of personality as it is learning to perceive life through expression. But still, life is all the same, a whole. There is only one, the all of it.

"If we were to collapse time and space in this particular moment, in this capsule of time and space, there would be nothing but the whole, the One. What would the One look like? The One would look like you and the One would look like me, all put together as energy from the Void.

"You and I are divided and individualized for experience only. As Soul, we live beyond dualities. When people learn to live as Soul and function in the world in that way, there cannot be any conflict, because only harmony exists within the whole. There cannot be any poverty, because poverty is a condition of one's mind. It is a state of consciousness. It is a viewpoint. As Soul, living as Soul, there is the viewpoint of Oneness of all things, therefore, there is abundance.

"If everything is One, then you, too, should enjoy abundance in all areas of life. You simply turn your attention towards that. There is nothing very confusing about it. You look at that in which you are interested and, because life is all Oneness, it then manifests. Now, this only works if you are living as Soul.

"If you are not viewing life as the whole, the moment you begin to compartmentalize life and say this is separate from that, and you take all your problems and try to pull them in separate directions to emotionalize over them, you have lost the capability of living Soul's abundant life.

"You and I are Soul. To live as Soul means that all life is One. Everything in life is for you and everything in life is for me. All we have to do is simply see it that way. We have to view life from the wholeness so that through the wholeness, we are able to decide and to make choices on the energy that we are perceiving. You are attracted to the energy in this direction. You look in that direction. You place your attention there, you reach for it, and it is yours.

"Now, 'yours'! What is yours? Since all life is a whole, we are only caretakers of everything. It is not your possession versus my possession. I am not saying that individually you don't own cars and houses and that kind of thing. Of course you do. But, as Soul, you still have that 360 degree viewpoint that, since all life is One, everything you own is a part of the whole; therefore, it is enriched by the wholeness of life, not only your own set of personality values.

"Enriched by the personality of life, then, we can interact with life as a whole; to give and to take, since giving is receiving and receiving is giving. You see how it goes full circle in anything that you try to talk about?

"This group of people, this Oneness, this circle that we are in right now is very advanced. Oneness has opened in you to the point where you are prepared to receive the idea that life is One, that we are living beyond dualities. If you were not prepared to receive this, you would not be able to receive the message.

15

"Later, you may break down these ideas in your mind, reviewing some of the words we have spoken here, and you may say to yourself, 'I don't know, this sounds rather frightening.' The 'little self' is starting to kick in and it says, 'But what if? I don't want to lose this little part of myself that I have come to cherish.' Please pay attention. You lose nothing as Soul. And I am saying this so that your minds are put at ease. *As Soul, there is nothing to lose.* You cannot lose your possessions as Soul, because, as Soul you are only caretakers of them. And this goes for the person who rejects this knowledge, as well. You might be the owner of a big corporation and say, 'Winged Wolf's statement does not apply to me', but it does apply to you, as well. I say to you now, to clarify this concept, *you are only a caretaker of your possessions!*

"As Soul, you can only move forward in all aspects of your life. You cannot be cheated out of anything. You cannot lose anything because everything belongs to the whole. If you lose an object and, if you are living beyond the dualities in the Oneness of all life, then that object will be returned to you, if it was useful in your life.

"Vibrations that you put on those things that are a part of your life, are glued to you. So, you are not going to lose anything. You don't give up anything by living as Soul, except an ego idea that says, 'I am different than everybody else'.

"I am no different from you. I have two arms; two legs; a nose and a mouth; two eyes; two ears. We are the same. I have a different set of nerve endings, or maybe they are operating a little differently in my brain than they are in your brain, because of my life experiences versus your life experiences; but, there still is no separateness. There is no 'this side versus that side' because the more one lives as Soul, the more integrated their brain is.

"*One gains the capacity to live in companion energy with all life, which is what Shaman Consciousness*

16

is - *Companion Energy*. The Shaman Consciousness has the capacity to live in harmony with all life. Since that consciousness perceives energy, it looks at something and understands it, or it looks at a person and understands that person. That is all.

"So, when you go to rest tonight and the ideas of the 'little self' come in to form conflict, do not say 'no' to it. Just listen and acknowledge its separateness. Run a little test on yourself. Listen to the arguments that come to you in the night. Listen to the arguments to determine their *separateness*.

"Yes, you can enjoy separateness in anything that you want, but do the arguments that are given to you for separateness, really exist? *Beyond dualities, separateness is an illusion.*

"We are a spiritual family on the brink of wakefulness. People are asleep and people are waking up. You are waking up. I want you to take a look at the idea of dualities; that there are none, and that separateness is an illusion.

"Are there any questions?"

*Questioner: "Winged Wolf, when the mind is bringing in separateness and you listen to it, will it then stop? Often my mind, when I listen to it, will keep at me from another angle, so I keep listening to it until it stops. What exactly do you do?"*

"When your mind starts talking to you and you are listening to it, use that listening time as a trigger into Soul Vision. Put your attention up here on the third eye. When you do, you will listen to it without any attachment whatsoever. Then it is almost like taking scissors and cutting the ribbon of thought. The 'little self' may kick in again and say, 'I'm afraid if that ribbon of thought is broken, I will become a vegetable?' Well, do I look like a vegetable? (laughs) I do not live like a vegetable. I live like a free individual."

Questioner: "If we are living as Soul, why do we need to communicate?"

"We are living in a physical body. Companion energy is very, very important. Since we are One, we communicate to bring that Oneness into harmony between us. When you attain Shaman Consciousness, we won't have to speak (Pause..) but we might just go ahead and play a lot. The play will be a totally different type of play than how we play now. This may be something that you are not able to picture at this time, and that doesn't matter. The type of play I am speaking of is play that is freedom; it is real play as Soul. But, communication is very important. We need to develop companion energy between each of us to communicate - to be friends, to laugh together, sometimes to cry together, and to recognize the Soul aspect of each other."

Questioner: "I had a question about how we, as a group, should communicate as Soul rather than speaking to each other about things each of us has done in the past."

"This is the Village of the Present Moment, isn't it? (referring to the theme of The Path of Soul™ Gathering.) So, in this village we are to stay as much as we can in the present. And, I set it up as a challenge for you to focus on NOW. In focusing on Now, what can you talk about? Well, you can talk about your prayer stick as you are making it. You can talk about your study groups as you are experiencing them. That kind of thing. What you are learning.
        "You know, the past can be viewed in several ways. In one way it is like a history book. You look at it and it contains facts of past events. It is very valuable

when you look at it in this way. However, if you have emotions attached to the history book, then the past is detrimental, because emotions are buttons -- anger and superficial joy and other illusionary type feelings. True feelings are the feelings of the present moment and those send body signals through you.

"Right now notice Stone Carver's stick. When she came and sat down next to me, she showed me that she had found a brilliant green dead bug on the ground. She glued it to her stick. That was being very present in the moment, to have that expired bug appear before her eyes. Do you see?

"People found feathers because they were present, in the moment. Sitting and looking at the ground, or looking out at the water, or gazing at the person across from you in the circle, you have a feeling of just being present - watching the smoke rise from the fire pit and float over the heads, the sound of a car passing in the distance, the crackling of the fire. You see, there are many things happening in this present moment. Pay attention to the movement of people within the circle, energy as it changes when movement occurs, people shifting to stretch their legs out, to sit up straight, to lean down.

"Be aware of the present moment. It holds so much. Sometimes you have to be still a little bit in the beginning. As you are walking somewhere, keep your focus on exactly where you are. Challenge yourself to see what is going on. Be aware of what the moment holds. Sight. Sound. Smells. The present is very full. Communicate that.

"People operating from a mental state of consciousness are always looking for something sensational to communicate. Real life is quite sensational. The finding of that little green bug that Stone Carver glued to her stick is quite sensational, as well as the movement of energy within life, because life actually transmutes energy.

"In shifting one thing, a domino effect occurs. One thing happens and then another thing happens, because of it. Slight movement creates change within the environment. So, there are plenty of phenomena, interesting things happening, if you slow yourself down to live in the present moment and take notice. *The present moment is an exalted state of consciousness.*"

*"You and I are divided and individualized for experience only. As Soul, we live beyond dualities."*

# LIVING WHOLEHEARTEDLY

**Winged Wolf:** "May the blessings be. (To Standing Turtle), "Did you go to Friday Harbor yesterday?"

*Standing Turtle: "Yes, I had a very good time."*

Speaking to Sky Wolf,

"What did you do yesterday?"

*Sky Wolf: "I went up Mt. Constitution, to the tower. There is a 360 degree view up there. Then, later, I went to the hot springs and sauna.*

"Maybe next year we can have Sky Wolf build a sauna on the property, by the pond. Wouldn't that be nice?"

*Standing Turtle: "Except for the mud."*

"Let's talk about that. If next year Sky Wolf could build a sauna, out on a little island in the pond, then after using it, we could take a dip in the pond. Would you then come along and say, 'Oh, but there is too much mud in the pond?' If there wasn't mud in the pond, would there be something else that was wrong with it? Do you see? No matter where you go, there is something about something that is never quite right. You have to remember this is the physical plane. So, everything is not quite right about everything.

"If you went to the hot springs, it would not be quite right because there are other people around. It is not quite right because of this. It is not quite right because of that. You say, 'Only if this were changed and that were changed, then it would be right.' But, it is never quite right. So, the idea is not to worry about the 'quite rightness' of it. Just enjoy it! The thing is, love the present moment.

"Give yourself a mud bath, then rinse off. The pond is full of clear water. In some areas it is a little cloudier than others but there are many areas that have deep pools that are not cloudy.

"The idea is not to worry about the little things in life. Do not worry about little inconveniences. When you decide to do something, do it wholeheartedly. Just know that it will be wonderful and enjoy it. Do not worry about 'what if this,' or 'what if that.' If there is something you want to do, do it! Or, if there is something you are supposed to do, do it!

"When I say, 'supposed to do', this is the idea. I'll give you an example. Suppose you have a job to do, such as setting up for the Gathering. Do not take the easy way, take the best way. Do not look for a short cut if the short cut begets a lesser result. Do the best you can, then the results come back in the best way.

"Always give your best to whatever you are doing. Do not say, 'Oh, this is not that important.' Everything is important, because everything exists in the present moment. The present moment has to be wholehearted. If it is not wholehearted, it comes out half-hearted, and half-heartedness gets half-hearted results. That is not the way of a Spiritual Warrior.

"I could have kept quiet this morning. I had no intention of talking, but we had to look at something, and so we looked at it. It is called wholeheartedness.

"Living wholeheartedly in the present moment is never counting on somebody else to pick up the slack. It is doing it yourself. When somebody might say, 'Hey, can I give you a hand over there?' Yes, you can! Or, you might ask, 'If you aren't doing anything, will you help me?' You can ask for help, but you do not count on it. You must be prepared to do everything yourself.

"Those having Shaman Consciousness are totally self-reliant. They do not expect to use the energy and assistance of others. They are prepared to do the whole thing themselves, wholeheartedly with joy, never begrudgingly.

"Work joyfully. Work is not something to dislike or avoid. Work is glorified movement of the body. Through it, we gain fluidity, health, and mental rest. It is what Alana called the DO in life. If your DO, your work or labor, is in harmony with the images you carry in your mind, then your DO becomes that which moves you ahead spiritually.

"Work is a gift of life. It is how to become a valuable contributor to life. Everything always goes full cycle, giving and receiving, or work, and the results of the work. It is a healthy circle, going and coming around. So you see, all of life commands our gratitude. When we live in this way, we become a spiritual being. We become empowered by everything we do.

"This is not to say that you give foolishly of yourself to everyone you meet. It is not to say that people should take advantage, because a Spiritual Warrior is never taken advantage of. A Spiritual Warrior makes conscious choices to do something. We are here on this property by conscious choice. I made my choice to be here. You made your choice to be here. Once a decision is made, give yourself to it, and give yourself to it wholeheartedly. In this ONEness, there is great joy and great freedom. Some day, you may be busy working somewhere else and you will not have an opportunity to be a part to the land Between the Wind, as you are now. And, that too, will be good in its own time, because then it will be the season to be somewhere else."

# OVERCOMING CONFLICT

**Winged Wolf:** "You have both done wonderful work on the Happy House, (which used to be a chicken house), and I want you to know how very much I appreciate you. When I came down here, I looked at the Happy House and it looked very different than it did before you started working on the inside. The energy you put on the inside shows on the outside. It is very special.

"It makes a big difference when someone cares on the inside because it shows on the outside, and that is what you have done with this chicken house. You are transforming it from the inside and it is glowing on the outside. It is a place of honor. It is a place where Soul is going to come into fruition by experiencing itself. It has a multiple purpose and its purpose is beginning to show.

"This is what is happening to both of you, as well. You carry a feeling for each other when you work closely together.

"Sometimes you feel resentful of one another. Most of the reason of the resentfulness is because you don't understand each other. Sky Wolf has trouble understanding because he can't hear, and Standing Turtle has trouble understanding because she can't understand his lack of hearing. I'm not saying that you are both not making an effort. I know you are but, it's that business of what's on the inside, shows on the outside.

"Even thinking miserable things about the other person shows on the outside. When one looks at this chicken house, one senses the changes are showing on the outside, as well. It is a perfect example.

"When you are uptight about something on the inside, about something that somebody has done, and you think angrily, it shows on the outside, even if you have not

24

said it. Your feelings and your thoughts have energy, so what you are feeling on the inside shows on the outside, *even if you say nothing.* The other person picks up on the energy of it, which is why it is so important.

"Balance follows resonance. Where things resonate together, the energy blends together. This is natural law. The energy of the inside of this chicken house has a natural flow to the energy of the outside. The energy of the inside of you, is the same as the energy on the outside.

"What you look like on the inside shows on the outside. How very important this is! What you are feeling inside of yourself, when you go out into the world, shows on the outside in energy that people pick up. How very, very important this is.

"So, as you walk along feeling that somebody is not understanding something, and you are feeling the pressure of it, what is happening is, they are feeling pressure from you and begin to build resentment in return, and they don't even know why, half the time.

"Do you see how important it is to live with a silent mind? You don't have to be thinking wonderful thoughts about somebody. If you do that, that will be misunderstood, as well. Balance is the result of having a silent mind. If you are under pressure, it is okay to say you are feeling under pressure. Release that pressure by talking about it, if you need to. Come and talk to me. You can always talk to me.

"It is okay to feel misunderstood sometimes. Everybody is misunderstood sometimes. That is part of being alive and being human. And isn't it wonderful to be so alive and to be so aware! It is okay. It's even okay to be wrong sometimes. It doesn't matter, if somebody else calls you wrong, or even if you know that you goofed. So what? Sometimes you can see where perhaps you didn't really goof, but you could have communicated a little better if you hadn't been impatient. And that goes for the one who doesn't hear, as well as the one who does hear. Do you see? It is the same thing. It is the same handicap even though a different handicap. *It is the same handicap, one who doesn't hear versus one who can't understand one who doesn't hear.* Do you see? It's just the other side of the coin.

"We are studying what is beyond dualities again. We want to shed dualities, because it's all one. Its all the same.

"So, be tolerant of each other, and in the tolerance let your mind fall silent. When you feel especially agitated, go somewhere and be still. Take a moment or two for yourself. You don't have to account for your minutes here. Go sit in the sunshine or go lie down and put your face on the wet grass. It doesn't matter that it is wet. You see? It feels good that it is wet. It makes a strong imprint of the present moment. It brings you back to the present.

"Put your nose in the earth and smell the earth. How lucky you are that you have the sense of smell, that you can see. Don't waste energy on things that don't matter.

"If something is troubling you, you can usually make it go away by lying down on the wet soil or by sticking a toe in the pond, by doing things that are out of the ordinary for yourself. The out-of-the ordinary helps you stay in the present moment. Do things out of the ordinary. Take your shoe off and stick your foot in the pond, then dry your foot off, put your sock back on, your shoe back on, and walk off. Nobody has to know. That's for you. Do things like that for yourself just to bring yourself sharply back into the present moment. Put a tarp down on the ground if you want and lie on the tarp. Reach your head out and put your face on the ground. Do anything for yourself that helps you stay in the present moment, anything except pain, that is.

"Don't ever inflict pain on yourself. Always make life's pictures as beautiful as you can make them. The prettier the pictures you put in your mind, the easier life is. Fill your brain with pretty pictures whenever possible. Putting your face onto blades of grass is wonderful. I've done it many times. Sometimes I do that in the middle of the night.

"Be alive to the moment, whatever the moment is. And, I have to tell you, I love this chicken house, this Happy House. This room is wonderful. Thank you. And, it's all teamwork. Maybe one person is doing most of the physical labor on it, but, the energy is teamwork. It's always working together.

"May the blessings be."

*"So, as you walk along feeling that somebody is not understanding something, and you are feeling the pressure of it, what is happening is, they are feeling pressure from you and begin to build resentment in return, and they don't even know why, half the time."*

# SPONTANEITY

**Winged Wolf:** "Today, we will be speaking about spontaneity. I do not have any thoughts going on in my head, yet, suddenly, words will come. This is spontaneity. Most people have a conditioned thinking process that puts a stream of words into their minds. They are looking at their words, putting the words together in their minds as they speak them.

"As Soul, you simply say the words as they appear, so there is no premeditation. It is a whole different process.

"Spontaneity and the way you are used to experiencing spontaneity, is different from spontaneity as Soul. Spontaneity as Soul, just *IS*. You just Do! There is no process to it. You bypass the process and act accordingly to what is called for in the moment.

"When I am working with apprentices, I don't premeditate how I am going to deal with them. Today, I know that when we are finished here, I am going to retrieve someone from a Vision Quest, but that is as far as it goes. I set some targets, just as you do in your life about your business, or personal situations, however, the manner in which I carry out everything is spontaneous.

"Spontaneity does not have anything to do with mental chatter or setting something up in a processed premeditated way. It simply is. Your difficulty is that your mind is continually working. You are thinking words and mentally chattering where you want to go with them. *Stop doing that!*

Sioux, Winged Wolf's wolf, positions herself between an apprentice and Winged Wolf, to be petted. The apprentice tries to move her away.

"You don't need to be so annoyed. If you were not so annoyed at Sioux standing in front of you right now, she would leave. It was your annoyance that created the glue to hold her. Whenever you place strong attention on something, you hold on to that which you have placed your attention. In fact, you attract it directly to you. So, just acknowledge her, then ignore her. Your ignoring vibes will release her. (Sioux goes over and stands by Winged Wolf). She knows she is being talked about right now, so she is standing next to me. She is thinking, 'Does this mean Winged Wolf is going to rub my chest?' She is testing it out with her body, but as soon as I change the subject, she will go to someone else.

"Spontaneity is kind of a tricky thing. What most people think of as spontaneous is not spontaneous. Their idea of spontaneity is when they have an itch, they scratch it. Now that is spontaneous, however in some places it might not be appropriate to scratch. (Laughs). Being spontaneous does not mean walking into a room belching or using crude language. If you are doing that, your refinement has not kicked into place. You would not be refined enough to exercise spontaneity and would, therefore, be better off without it. At that point, mind chatter is actually preferable.

"If you are going to injure another person with your spontaneity, there is an imbalance within yourself. None of you do that, but it is important to mention it, because that is always a question that somebody will ask, 'Is it spontaneous to hit somebody, if provoked?' No, it is not. Only a very warped core of intelligence operates like that. Rough behavior does not come from Soul. When anything comes from Soul, it is never aberrant."

Two Eagles: "So does 'spontaneity' seem to be tempered with appropriateness?"

29

"If your spiritual refinement is intact, it will automatically be tempered with appropriateness. This is really important to remember. When I am dealing with you, my speech and actions are always appropriate, even if I am being silly. And that is because I am being silly as Soul. So if you can learn to eliminate the mental chatter that sets up your spontaneity, real spontaneity will kick into place. You can do that more and more by just being centered at the Third Eye.

"So you see, spontaneity is not what you thought it was. Soul naturally refines the personality. One of the first things Soul does is to quiet the mind, bringing Soul into operation, then spontaneity can just *BE*. But there are several degrees of stilling the mind. It takes awhile for one's mental chatter to settle down to a Soul level. In the beginning, it will quiet down a little bit here, and then it's noisy, and then it quiets again, and then it's noisy and then it quiets again, etc.

"Speaking from Soul level, where the mind is actually still and, where what comes out of your mouth, or what goes into your actions, is premeditated only in the sense that you know where you are going. For example, I know when I go into the office I am going to do certain things, perhaps I am going to write an article, perhaps I am going to answer mail. So, I know only approximately what I will do, but I do not think about how it will be carried out ahead of time. I just sit down and do it, now in the present moment.

"If I were to consider an article I wanted to write, I would *look* at the idea without any mental comment. I would simply *look* at it, feel the energy of it and then spontaneously write it. The more I felt the energy of it, the more I would draw companion energy from the environment to get the job done. When I *look* at an article that I want to write about Soul, I have strings of energy attached to all of you and to all the apprentices that are everywhere out there. So, when *looking* at an article or *looking* at the energy of what I need to do, that companion energy provides what I need to know, because we are all one. There is no separateness. That level of us is all one. You still have your individuality but *we are all One*, which makes it very special.

"This is where you come into knowledge belts, which will show you anything you want to know. You can only do this as Soul, from being centered at the Third Eye.

"When you come to a certain point in your spontaneous development as Soul, the energy runs through your body and you call on it at will. This is accomplished not by words 'come to me energy', but flushing the energy right through your body.

"If you do that too many times in a day, it is difficult to settle down. You will want to jump out of your skin. It is spontaneous when it is called upon. *Looking* is very different from thinking as you are used to doing. *Looking* is a very natural way of operating. You simply look.

"You can *look* with your eyes, but a blind person can *look* too. You can *look* with your ears but a deaf person can *look* with ears too. You can *look* with your body. Every cell in your body is a part of *looking*. That is why a healthy body is so useful.

"When the mental chatter is gone, you are still evolving in the process of living as Soul. The mental chatter is the first great division. When the mental chatter stops, there is a whole other world AS SOUL that you experience, and that whole other world has multiple dimensions within it. It is unlimited where you can go and I have only begun to tap it.

"As you are moving along, different things become apparent that were not there before. As you yield to the Void and become more and more *IT*, even though you are *IT* 100% wholeheartedly, the Void is evolving. The Void is constantly evolving, God is constantly evolving, and the evolution of this process is limitless, which means where you go as Soul is such that what you begin to take into your life becomes something that you could not possibly premeditate. Spontaneity would suddenly roll the energy through your body or pluck some kind of nectar out of the environment, not as a knowledge belt but as an energy resource. But this process is **never** premeditated.

"Demands upon someone as they move along, living as Soul, become greater, but in a very relaxed way so that, that which is available to you is greater. The more the demand, the more you can access. The more the demand, the more you are willing to give and you are giving the Void Itself.

"Spontaneity really has nothing to do with what the dictionary says spontaneity is and yet it does. The dictionary would probably define spontaneity as, 'A remark of the moment, or movement of the moment', which indeed it is. But, as Soul, this present moment becomes so huge, so magnanimous, so macrocosmic, because the Void is constantly expanding. It is always moving to that new level. It is astounding.

"What you want to do is to give yourself more and more to that Third Eye center. When I say give yourself to it, I mean give your attention to it and watch the mind as you go about it. Be aware of when the mind kicks in to talk to you to set up the next moment.

"You have been letting it run the show for a long time and a big piece has let go, but when it totally lets go, you will slip into another world and that is when the *real journey as Soul begins!* It is not that far off for any one of you. What is really holding you back most of the time is your mind. It will kick in and it will look at what it is doing and it will say, 'I don't know if I can do this', and you get frightened. You scare yourself off. Or you say, 'Oh, where am I going? It is so beyond me'. Well, it is not beyond you! It is your birthright. It is You. You are becoming more you, not less you. You are becoming You."

"Spontaneity really has nothing to do with what the dictionary says spontaneity is and yet it does. The dictionary would probably define spontaneity as, 'A remark of the moment, or movement of the moment', which indeed it is. But, as Soul, this present moment becomes so huge, so magnanimous, so macrocosmic, because the Void is constantly expanding. It is always moving to that new level."

# CREATION

**Winged Wolf:** "All things are created by the energy of that which dreams it. We call it presentation, because actual creation is already finished, in that the bits and pieces of creation are finished. Creation is a misused word. Presentation is more accurate.

"Creation itself is a word to apply to something coming from nothing, the Void being nothing and the dreamer being something. The dreamer dreams the nothing into being something.

"Everything is creation. Again, out of the nothing the dreamer dreams something. All the atoms and molecules come together to make something fashioned through the image of the dreamer.

"The dreamer has to be careful not to manipulate the atoms and molecules because, when somebody does that, there is a mishap. It never quite works. Void energy does not respond to manipulation, except by responding in chaos, so you have to meet the energy as the dreamer without manipulation.

"Many people in the New Age community have the feeling that creative visualization is what makes creation. This is true as long as there is no manipulation to it. This means there is no conjuring of images. There is no *trying* involved.

"As Soul, we carry within us the seeds of everything that we ever wanted and those we ever will want. All you have to do is to set your sights on a target and then that target begins to come into fruition, just through being there, because the energy of Soul is the same as the energy of the Void. You, as Soul, are the dreamer. You dream those images into being without conjuring, in other words, without consciously trying to dream a situation to fit your 'little self' idea. Whenever the personality gets too far involved, the personality being the 'little self', is in control. When that happens the dream itself becomes distorted and aberrated in much the same way the 'little self' exists.

"Every person has a 'little self', a personality. Those who are controlled by that personality will find that their dreams match their personality. In other words, a personality has buttons and aberrations to it, which mixed together, becomes a hodge podge that is out of balance.

"Now, when you are living as Soul, you still have a personality, or a 'little self', but the personality or 'little self' does not dominate you, because when you go to manifest or create something through your dreaming, whatever it is that you carry inside of you, IS. You do not get a distorted image of what you want, because you do not manipulate.

"Because the Void cannot respond to manipulation without chaos, anytime you try to make things happen, atoms and molecules are stirred up in opposing directions. What was going on in circular fashion, now is going on in broken chaotic fashion, every which way. A little part may still be going on in circular fashion, but it is knocked out of balance and contorted.

"So you learn to *present* as Soul, remembering *'presenting'* has nothing to do with visualization. For example, some people who use visualization, put a dollar bill on the mantel and visualize many dollar bills but, because they are manipulating the energy, that visualization may materialize in them becoming a bank teller. Consequently, they end up having many dollar bills around them, but they are not in their own pocket.

"Another example of one's visualization backfiring, that we commonly hear about, is the way one tries to attract a lover. You visualize a person coming at you. Well, that person may come to you, but perhaps not for the reason you wanted. He may want to sell you something or perhaps ask you about going out with your

35

girlfriend. You see? Visualization often brings about circumstances that are chaotic and mixed up. To develop your life through visualization can be fruitless and disappointing.

"If you have a business venture that you want to go after, go after the business venture as Soul. Be centered at the Third Eye. Let it unfold itself. Don't push. Don't shove. Keep your attention on what you want and take the necessary steps to achieve your goal. It is your attention that brings the Void into the order, which presents what you want.

"Difficulty occurs when you become too busy. When you take your attention off one thing to put it on another, that which you took your attention off of, very often stands still. It is not meant for us to be so busy that our attention cannot be fused with what we are doing, but we do it in our society because we are moving so quickly. Are there any questions?"

*Gazelle: "Abundance is one of the things I have been wanting to bring into my life. I have just been looking and.."*

"Remember, abundance comes in many forms. You are speaking of money but abundance does not always mean money. So be specific.

"Abundance can be abundance of joy. It can be abundance of beauty or it can be abundance of something you do not want, as well. Do you see? Abundance is abundance. You gain abundance when you live as Soul; you gain the beauty of life when you live as Soul. The more you live as Soul the more abundance you gain. I have to say this in many different ways so that many different people can understand. I also say it many different ways so that your mind can understand it many different ways, because you are listening with your mind and your mind sets up conflict. Your mind is analyzing what I am telling you.

"Abundance comes in many different packages. When you have abundance, you have it all. Money is a part of life. There is no reason you should not have abundance of money, as well. Abundance does not necessarily mean a million dollars, but it means being comfortable in your finances, as well as in other areas, with enough extra to finance what you want to do.

"There is another ingredient involved, and that is the step you must take to earn it. This is the physical plane. Money does not fall out of the sky, although it may. For example, you may inherit money, or you win the lottery. But this is not the usual way of acquiring abundance for a person living as Soul. These are karmic flukes, in other words, you have so much karma stored up in a financial area that money will come to you. You see? A clog that stuck way back in a past existence, may suddenly click into place and the synchronicity of the moment brings the lotto ticket to fruition.

"This is not the kind of abundance we are talking about, is it? We are talking about abundance that multiplies in your life. If you have a job that pays you a set amount of money, it can be very difficult to increase that amount. However, many people on the Path of Soul get into areas of self-employment, because they become very innovative in their life style. This is not to say that everybody should be self-employed. It just opens the door to do different things, to expand here and there, whereas if you are working for someone else, you may be held back by company policy. When you are self-employed, the bureaucracy might be waiting on the fringes, but your own innovativeness, and presentation of what you are doing usually bypasses that. So, we are talking about freedom.

"You, Gazelle are an excellent special education teacher. I would not want to discourage you from teaching. Do you see? You have a real gift. Maybe you could do some tutoring on the side, which would bring the extra money you want.

"It is always best, if you want to do something extra, to do it in a field you like. To work at something you do not like, becomes drudgery. If you get a part-time job working in a grocery store, when what you really want to be doing is teaching, you cut yourself down by stepping into drudgery. 'Oh, I have to do this and I don't want to.' A person living as Soul never does what they do not want to do, except to get out of bed at a certain time, but even that is a choice.

"Align your action with your dreams and that will give you the abundance you need, the extra to fulfill the areas of your life that you want. Make note: Your reward will equal the degree of your expended energy.

*Two Eagles: "If I'm living my dream and there's an accident, am I responsible?"*

"Perhaps through your attitudes about what is going on, and through your opinions over somebody else's attitudes, you presented a situation. Your attitude is out there. When you have an attitude or an opinion while you are speaking to someone, or while you are interacting with someone, even though it is unsaid, the other person picks up on that. They hear it in their energy body and that is what they are responding to. So, yes, you do *present* it. You brought about that situation yourself."

*Two Eagles: "That is a lot of responsibility."*

"It is indeed! When you have a quiet mind and you approach someone in business or in any other situation, you have no attitudes or opinions, so the other person automatically feels comfortable. If others are  conniving to set up some situation in a manipulative fashion, you can perceive the energy and can make your choices of 'Yes, I want to', or 'No, I don't want to'. You do not become victimized as Soul and, therefore, you do not present a situation that you do not want.

"The magic of life occurs when you have a quiet mind. That is where freedom resides. You can be talking to anybody about anything and, if your mind is quiet, you do not present any conflict to them. In other words, you do not present any strong opinions or attitudes that they have to resist. Therefore, they have a choice of accepting or rejecting your proposal and vice versa. It is a clean working situation.

*Two Eagles: "If I notice the behavior of someone that I do not like or I have a thought or a judgment about it, as long as I do not focus on that judgment and just notice, does it have the same impact?"*

"No, it does not have the same impact. You can look at something as Soul, your mind is quiet and so you can see what is going on. If you can feel an abrasiveness in your body, somebody is doing something that is not appropriate for a situation. The abrasiveness is a signal to pay attention. If you see a situation that is evolving and your body feels an abrasiveness, act immediately. Take the moment in hand. Talk to people as Soul. Talk to them, not to clear the air, but to express what it is that you are feeling. Let them know that you are perceiving something and do it in everyday language. You do not have to get into esoteric principles. Be very straight about it.

"If, in the meantime, as you are looking at how to deal with the situation, that person picks up on the energy and makes the correction, you do not have to speak up. You must begin to take the step to correct the situation, not to change it. Changing it would be manipulation. Trying to change the way someone else thinks is manipulation.

"If you are an employer, and have many people working for you, they have to conform to your mold of the dream. It is your dream and they are paid to act within it. As an employee you might resent this bureaucracy, but the bureaucracy pays your paycheck and you have made an agreement to work for it. If you are an employee, you have to *do it* your employer's way and be impeccable about it. Give 100% of yourself to your work."

*"As Soul, we carry within us the seeds of everything that we ever wanted and those we ever will want. All you have to do is to set your sights on a target and then that target begins to come into fruition, just through being there, because the energy of Soul is the same as the energy of the Void."*

# PARALLEL WORLDS
## Part One

**Winged Wolf:** "Parallel time occurs in the astral plane, which has many, many, many, many, many dimensions, countless dimensions, dimension within dimension, within dimension, within dimension. Basically, however, the astral plane is broken down into zones. These divisions were invented by religions to try to explain the nature of these zones. Hindu, Muslim, Buddhists, and other Eastern religions did this. The astral plane is comprised of the causal zone, an area where all information from past lives is stored, and there is also the mental zone where ideas give rise to mental inventions.

"Basically you have what is called the astral plane, however, all dimensions are included here. The astral plane is a plane of existence where emotions propel ideas and propel art. At the top of the astral plane is the etheric zone, which is the zone of intuition. Intuition is the final dimension within the astral plane before one steps over the invisible line into the territories of Soul. Since it exists closest to the Soul plane, the etheric zone is the first message body that Soul uses to communicate. This is the zone where intuitional hunches come from.

"As parallel worlds, these particular areas - causal, mental, intuitional - are a part of the astral plane and many dimensions are contained in each of them. We could break these zones into smaller and smaller dimensions but we are not going to do that. However, we are going to note those divisions so that you can understand what they are all about.

"When something occurs in the astral plane it is reflected here in the physical plane and that occurrence could have something to do with you. When you have a

41

sudden burst of emotion, that emotion occurs first on the astral plane, and then here. Actually, it occurs simultaneously, but according to most spiritual teachings, it happens first there and then here. This is where 'as above so below' comes from. It is really simultaneous because, you see, there is no division between here and there. Here and there are the same thing and, when you really grasp the idea that here and there are the same thing, then you will no longer look at here and there as over there by the pond versus here in the Happy House. When you *really* grasp this, you are free to explore dimensions without movement, but with movement, a similar idea to the art of doing without doing.

"You simply are where you want to be. Some teachings say that the shift is merely a movement in consciousness. It is actually more than that. It is *awareness* that makes it possible and not so much a shift in consciousness. Your awareness causes the shift.

"We are not talking about intellectual awareness. When you get to a certain point in your development as Soul, your intellect becomes integrated with you, as Soul, then whatever it is that you perceive equals NOW. So, you see, the parallel planes are not really running along side each other. They are really One, seemingly parallel, seemingly outside, seemingly above, and seemingly below. You, as Soul, will perceive them as one.

"When you are 'looking', pulling in images from the astral plane into this plane, the image may have nothing in particular to do with the physical plane. They may be merely remnants of life energy that lived once around here. So, what you are doing, is pulling in astral imprints that were left in the environment. Those imprints are invisible, until they are perceived; and they are perceived by someone who is sensitive to that type of thing and that is usually one who possesses raven medicine.

"Raven medicine does not draw in entities from the astral plane, but it can see the imprints of what has been. But allow this sight to occur naturally. Never draw in astral entities. Never draw in astral entities. Never, never, never NEVER draw in astral entities. Stay within your own reality. By staying in your own reality you will not get caught up in confusion of what is outside of your reality and make somebody's facsimile your reality.

"This is where people get into trouble. They get into trouble as *channels*. They get caught up in somebody else's reality because they have deliberately drawn upon astral forces, alien astral forces. Now, I am not referring to aliens from another planet, however, that could be applied as well, because those entities from another planet also exist in the astral plane, many of them. Some have refined bodies and it is borderline. Aliens actually have a body type combination.

"To attract entities who are still hanging around in the astral plane after they have translated or died, maybe a thousand years ago, is something else. They are still hanging around for whatever reason. They would like to find a way to come back to life but they cannot seem to, because somehow or another their karma does not line up and they cannot get drawn back into physical life. So know that entities are waiting out there when you start fishing, 'Oh, is there a spirit guide there for me? Can somebody help me?'. Do you see? They are waiting to jump right in and, as soon as they do, they can easily, through trickery, take command of your body. Obviously, they cannot get a body and that is why they want to use somebody else's, to express themselves through that body. That is how important this physical body is. It is a vehicle for God Consciousness. Don't give your power away to anyone or anything!

"Knowledge alone cannot be bought or sold like that. It is like making a bargain, a bargain with the astral entity. 'You teach me and you can use my body'. Well, you might learn something but you will not be able to exper- ience it, to act it out. The astral entity will get to act it out instead. Do you see the difference? Don't mess with it. You are really playing with danger and it may throw you to the other side, into the astral entity's space, which means you become trapped on the other side. Then, because you have given up your body and your personal power, you take on the astral entity's karma. Do you see how dangerous channeling is? It is fiercely dangerous! You take on the astral entity's karma and become discarnate. *Don't give up your power to anyone or anything.* That is too big a price. You lose your life and you are wandering bodiless for who knows how long? However, maybe that entity's karma is suddenly going to line up and it's going to come back into a physical body, but, maybe it isn't. And, why do you want to live out their karma anyway? What kind of karma did they have to be without a body so long?

"You know Adolf Hitler had the God knowledge. He abused the God knowledge. Adolf Hitler is still in the astral plane. He has not been able to accept a body, because every time he accepts a body, he is squashed, he is dead. See? He is really and truly, sincerely working to turn his karma around now, but it is a slow process. Too many people remember. As soon as he is born, he is a still birth, or the nurse drops him on the floor, or he is born into an abusive family and murdered by his parents, or suffocates in a car, or whatever. Do you see? He has not been able to even live six months in any form, bug or otherwise.

"If you let an entity, who has not been able to accept a human body, take control of your body, it will quickly destroy your body, because the energy is alien to your body. I do not want to use names, but one well known channeler recently shriveled into an arthritic ball. Her body simply disintegrated.

"It is not uncommon. A woman visited me at Eastcliffe in Cottonwood who was a well-known channeler. She had elephantiasis in her legs and the affliction began when she opened herself to channel the entity. Her health was continuing to go downhill and so, I said, 'You will have to give it up'. 'I'll do it', she answered, but she could not do it. Do you see? She was taken over. There was too little time that the entity allowed her to make use of her body; so little time. There was no way she could have given it up.

"People do not know what they are doing with this channeling business. It is not that what the entities say is not wonderful. Often it is wonderful. Truth is always wonderful to hear, but those who accept the entity are giving away their bodies, their right to life and they are taking on the entities karma.

"Remember, there is always a reason someone is trapped in the astral plane. It is really a privilege to be able to manifest a body and to be able to live a life. The more harmonious the life, the stronger and healthier the life force. We are talking about productivity. The more refined the dream, the more refined your life is. Do not let somebody interfere with that and mess it up for you. You get in there and take responsibility for yourself. Do not give your power away. It is so, so important for people to understand this.

"I am not saying entities are bad. You cannot blame someone being trapped on the other side waiting to find a way in. Some are doing 'good' work but there are other ways of getting that work done. It is best if they go ahead and earn their own bodies first and do that work in the bodies that they earn, bodies they are able to manifest. Otherwise, the entity's karma controls the individual who allows the entity to use their body, and that karma then becomes present on the Earth. It becomes present on the physical plane. That karma, that did not allow them to manifest, is now living, expressing itself in life. The fact that the entity says good things is not the point.

"So, there is a mixture of the good things, isn't there? It is a little bit of a perversion of the good thing. How does that perversion affect our lives? Well, I have a book titled, *The Mind of Adolf Hitler*. Some of it is quite beautiful. He understood life, but there was a perversion there. I am not saying this is the case with all astral entities, but I am saying that there is a reason that they cannot incarnate and that reason, while they are using somebody else's body, is being expressed in the world. It is not healthy, not for you and me, not for the entire environment. It is polluting the environment. Stop It!"

(To Ravenwolf)

"Astral or emotional imprints of translated beings that you saw in nature are everywhere. Everywhere. Seeing them is a gift. That is being a seer. You were looking into the ethers and you were seeing life as it was in a past time. The images came to you. Through those images, you were able to understand some of your own existence, but they are not related. What you saw were not live images. They were merely imprints, intense episodes of people's lives. If you go into an old church, you may feel the sorrow, weeping and wailing, which once occurred at a communion rail over a death, or something traumatic. Churches are often filled with grief. When you can walk into a church and sit down quietly, you may see a flash, an image, or you may be overcome with a sense of mourning. When this occurs, you are being touched by an emotional (astral) imprint left behind.

Raven medicine says you have the ability to perceive these imprints. Most people have a little bit of

46

raven medicine. You (Ravenwolf) have a little bit more. It is nothing particularly to develop or not to develop, but, to wait and see what it is. Do not push at things to invite problems. I will work with you on that. It can be very useful. It is another way of perceiving energy and a very powerful way, because you get to see the actual picture of it, not just rely on your body to tell you.

"But, that is not really a parallel world, is it? All life is here and now, this moment! The entire astral plane is wrapped in this moment. This is the moment of Soul. The astral plane is merely a place with a lesser vibration than Soul.

"You have each done something very special to dream the bodies that you have and to dream your moment of being here. You are reaching for conscious awareness as Soul. That is a big deal to have dreamed yourself to that point, where you are recognizing who you are. That is a BIG DEAL!

"So, even though you went through all those experiences in your life to get here, seemingly almost lifetimes in between, somehow or another you got yourself steered into this position. It is quite an accomplishment!"

# PARALLEL WORLDS
## Part Two

**Winged Wolf:** "What did you see while we were HUing from the Third Eye chakra?"

*Ravenwolf: "Shadows."*

"Yesterday we described parallel worlds as imprints of feelings. Today we are going to talk about climate and what we present within the environment when we are doing different things.

"Our actions, the sounds we make, the words we speak, and the thoughts we have, present a climate around us, an environment. This environment is animated by atoms and molecules that move around within it. The climate we present actually adapts to shapes, according to what is going on inside of us. Some of those shapes are from our own aura, some are from our physical associations, and some shapes are attractions from the astral plane.

"Your own aura, of course, is your astral body. So, when we say 'you attract from the astral plane', we are saying your astral body is attracting beings and entities identical to the emotions you are living out on the physical plane.

"Remember, entities in the astral plane do not have a body through which to express themselves so they use earth bodies. (We are speaking of astral level not Soul level.) So, entities use other bodies to express themselves. If some entity has a weakness for alcohol, they literally hang near and vicariously enjoy the experience through you. Entities who were smokers may actually encourage you to light up at times when you hadn't thought of it. With any addiction or obsessive behavior you will find that an astral entity is

48

close by to enjoy the experience through you. Their enjoyment comes by sucking the nectar of your addiction through your own astral body. This sometimes makes it more difficult to give up an obsessive habit. When you have an obsessive habit, like alcohol, the entities that are used to hanging around you, are thirsty for it, as well. So, you find a little bit of encouragement to go against what you have decided to give up. Do you see? It is not Joe or Dick entity, not personification so much, as it is the craving energy. So, by studying, in parallel worlds, we are sticking our heads through the veil of life and looking at different aspects.

"This morning when we sat here and HUed, there were many, many images of entities forming around us. Some of them had body shapes, some of them did not. Some of them were from our own auras and others were not.

"I have many students on the astral plane just as I have many students here in the physical plane. Some of these forms joining us now are my students; some of them are not. They were attracted to our HUing song. Just as you and I in a physical body are attracted to it, they are also attracted.

"So, whatever we say or do as Soul, is not only heard and felt by other physical beings, but it is heard by those in the parallel worlds of the astral. What impact you have upon life itself! To attract the company you want in life, make your energy pure. Remember, 'like attracts like'.

"You attract friends in life according to your mental attitudes and your beingness, do you see? Likewise, you attract astral beings around you who are in harmony with who you are. How wonderful! What a thrilling adventure this is.

"You should not try to personify those beings who are around you. 'Oh! There's Joe over there in his light body. Come on in Joe. Come on in and sit down.' No, you are crossing a line when you do that. Do not do that. Acknowledge the presence and leave the personification alone, otherwise you are going to draw in other types of things. It is a very fine line here. If you cross over that line you are going to get into channeling and then you will enliven something that begins to get into your space. Be careful.

"There is another aspect of all this. You hear societies around the world, especially the New Age society talking about angels. Angels are real. They are people who live as Soul and they are astral beings who live as Soul. Now, there are beings in the astral plane who are learning to live as Soul, just like there are here, but the final living as Soul comes about in a physical body. So, beings on the other side who are attracted to you, and watching, are learning through your actions, through your quietness as Soul. If they are focused on you as Soul, they will be attuned to living as Soul, even though they are not in a physical body. And, when they are drawn back into life, situations will help them perpetuate what they have started in the astral plane. Do you see? They may be drawn back into life with a family that lives as Soul or will give them that opportunity. They are drawn back into life into a higher state of consciousness.

"Some of those beings, because they may be near you, may feel like an invisible buddy, but never forget, you are the leader of the friendship. You are the stronger energy. You are the energy that has the power to manifest a body and to be on the Path of Soul. The astral entity is on the Path of Soul through you and through the energies of others with whom they associate. You are on the Path because of your own readiness. You are the leader in the relationship. Never yield your energy to their energy. *Never Yield Your Energy To A Disembodied Energy. Never.*

"Do not think astral beings know more than you do. They do not. Now, I say, 'they do not', but they do. You may find that they have a rapport with you whether or not you have a rapport with them. You may get in some kind of danger and that astral being will do something to warn you of the pending danger. But, you can't always say warnings come from astral beings, because you are attached to whomever you have strings of energy with, such as someone who has a stronger life force than yourself, like myself.

"When I say I am always with you, I am ready to protect you, if you are walking the Path of Soul, do you see? Because I am the stronger energy, you can call on me. That does not mean you will always use me as a crutch, because you are becoming empowered, but it is better to call on me than to call on some unknown being, who has a lesser energy than you. Call on power, not someone who is aspiring to power.

"This view of parallel worlds broadens into subjects that are difficult to talk about, because of people's mind-set about them. Many people are looking for an invisible companion who will do everything for them. Somebody who lives from such a mental state is inviting possession or so-called channeling, and this is very dangerous. Their health will fail. Their outer life will fail. Entities are not equipped to run someone's life. They destroy life, not necessarily through maliciousness, but through lack of companion energy. They are not you. This is your body! You manifested it! You created it, so to speak. You presented it! This is yours, this body. Touch your faces. Really! Get the idea cemented in you: YOU MADE THIS!

"This body you presented for yourself has the capacity to live a certain amount of time, however you have to constantly be attuned to it, to keep it in harmony and health. Today the length of time we live in the ordinary world is about eighty to ninety years, sometimes more.

There is no reason, for example, that anybody has to contract Alzheimer's disease. Maintain nutrition and take vitamins. Watch your health.

"In the parallel worlds, you are the leader, not the disembodied entity. Appreciate the fact that throughout your life, you are nurturing those who do not have a body. Nurture them as Soul but do not nurture them with nicotine, drugs, or anger habits. Do not attract entities around you who have had the habits of flying into a rage. They will only help you perpetuate your own anger through their hunger to express it. The more you express anger and rage, the more satisfied they feel. Remember, these are entities without a body. They use other bodies as expressions but they have no right to do that. Instead, they could observe the greater energy and learn from it, to learn from you as Soul. Any questions?"

*Standing Turtle: "Would you compare the Void to the Astral Plane?"*

"All life is the Void. The Void is nothing and the Void is everything. The astral plane is a part of the Void just like physical life is a part of It. The astral plane is a finer form, the physical plane is denser, but denser does not mean lesser, because it takes energy and power for one to manifest in the physical plane. That which is stuck in the astral plane does not have that power to manifest as yet. That is why I say, you are the greater energy. All life is the Void.

"All life is the Void but entities living in the astral plane do not live from Void consciousness or God/Soul consciousness. That is only achieved in physical life, however, very few people in physical life live as Soul, so very few people live from Void or God consciousness, do you see?"

52

*Standing Turtle: "Where do those who live as Soul go after they translate?"*

"Those who live as Soul translate outside of time and space. There is no space and there is no time, it is all right here, now! There is no where to go. You are talking about a subject that, to discuss it, you have to remove all words. It is in the energy itself. It is pure consciousness. It is ultimate awareness. It is nowhere and it is everywhere."

*Standing Turtle: "Where do they reside?"*

"Who are you trying to personify as the Void?"

*Standing Turtle: "Jesus."*

"There are many imprints of Jesus on Earth. When I say 'many' I do not mean multitudes. People who live as Soul have imprints of Jesus, imprints of Buddha, imprints of Mohammed and imprints of anyone else who has ever lived as Soul because that is what the Void is, Soul."

*Standing Turtle: "Are we speaking of Shaman Consciousness?"*

"The Shaman Consciousness bears the same imprint as the Christ Consciousness, Buddha Consciousness, or the Mohammed Consciousness. 'Shaman' is a word that depicts consciousness. Shaman is also a word that is very misused in our society today. In most New Age circles, Shaman means witch doctor, sorcerer, game player and so forth. A Shaman is anything but that.

"The God Consciousness does not manipulate; therefore, the Shaman Consciousness does not manipulate and is not capable of sorcery. That does not mean it is not capable of power, it is very powerful, because it is not capable of sorcery. Power occurs naturally. People may think the Void Consciousness is extraordinary, but it is not.

It only appears extraordinary, because from where someone sits in their state of conflict, everything looks magical, but to someone who is living clearly as Soul, there is no such thing as extraordinary."

*"People do not know what they are doing with this channeling business. It is not that what the entities say is not wonderful. It is wonderful. Truth is always wonderful to hear but those who accept the entity are giving away their bodies, their right to life and they are taking on the entities karma."*

# ASTRAL IMPRINTS

**Winged Wolf:** "May the blessings be.

"When somebody dies, they sometimes hang around people they love for so long that they become glued to the survivors within that family circle. After a time, certain traits show up in a particular member, and she or he become more and more like the deceased.

"This has nothing to do with 'possession,' it has to do with a personal love bond, so it is very common to share bodies in that way."

*Standing Turtle: "Where is the Soul?"*

"The individuality of Soul is expressed through personality, but we are really all one. For each one of us, as we allow Soul to express itself through us, we become individualized as Soul. But, Soul itself is not individualized. God is one; God is a whole. As bits and pieces of God come down into the world of matter, and that is what Soul is, each becomes individualized. The personality, or that which has expressed itself in the world of matter, leaves imprints everywhere. The imprint of a parent can stay very strongly with one and that trait may develop in the individual still alive."

*Standing Turtle: "How would you relate that to the karma of the individual who left the imprint?"*

"Imprints left by famous persons through history, who have touched many lives, live on in people who are attracted to them through recorded history. These people build up scenarios within their own minds. Hitler, for example, left a tremendous imprint on the world. People feel hate and all kinds of ugliness toward him, because they remember the ugliness that was done. Those people who were carriers of that hate and ugliness, who are dying off, have passed their feelings on to other people. The second generation has it passed on to them as a weakened strain. So, it will get weaker and weaker.

"Jesus Christ left a great imprint in his followers. His followers kept spreading it out, and spreading it out, and spreading it out, until the imprint became a World Religion. Do you see? This imprint has been perpetuated two thousand years, which is pretty amazing. The same is true of Shãkyamuni Buddha, only longer.

"When someone aspires to that particular consciousness, the imprints from those spiritual teachers are accepted into the karma of the individual, and they begin to become like them, as well. That is what the Christ Consciousness is, or the Buddha Consciousness. You attain that consciousness by merging with that consciousness."

*Standing Turtle: "I am wondering how this affects an individual's karma?"*

"When you die, or translate, your children remember you. 'Translate' is a better word than 'die' because that is what death really is, a translation from one body into another body; a leaving of the body behind or a transmutation of energy to where the body no longer exists. Your children remember you in the way they loved you the most. In the beginning, some of your children might be angry at you for dying, but gradually that will fade, then they remember that which they loved most about you. These traits become alive in them. Your aliveness carried on in their memory in a way that their children will learn about you, and it will be carried on.

"Now it becomes an embellished version of who you were, because it is their interpretation. You see? It is

56

not only you, but it is you expressed through them in an embellished version. They put aside their own images because their own images are not as great. Then they carry this imprint on as an ancestry. That is how you perpetuate yourself."

*Standing Turtle: "Where am I now?"*

"Where are you? Well, it depends on your state of consciousness. If you remember in two of your apprentice journeys, you studied life and death, and what happens when you die. The reason you studied that was so you would recognize your moment of death, when it comes. A person's life is very, very important, yet the moment of death takes on a nature of its own, a consciousness. A person can live an entire life in elevated consciousness and fall. If they fall when the moment of death occurs, that is the consciousness with which they work and where they begin. So, the moment of death is very, very important.

"The upliftment of life as you are living it, is to be continued, do you see? It is a practice for the moment of death. Always bear this in mind if you are around someone who is dying. Do everything you can at that moment, even though they may have been horrible in life, to get them into an elevated state of consciousness, even if it is only for a moment. This is important, because that is the consciousness they are going to work with when they translate.

"That does not mean they can jump into Buddha Consciousness by focusing on Buddha, but they can get prepared for enlightenment in the next lifetime. It is like the story of the butcher who dies thinking about slaughtering sheep. He will wake up in the dream world of afterlife, dreaming about slaughtering, and that is how he is going to come back into life. So, it is better to be thinking about something uplifting and move forward."

# ENERGY

**Winged Wolf:** "We are going to talk about energy and its effects. When you have your mind going in many different directions, such as looking at pictures of things in your mind, of things you have to do, you are at the same time directing your movements outside of yourself. What happens is, you are very scattered.

"When you are scattered like that, everything that you touch has a chaotic result. The chaotic result will show up in all kinds of funny little ways. (To Leaping Dear) Like last night, you were standing, talking to me in the kitchen and every time I tried to open up a vitamin capsule to put into the dog food, the capsule would fly out of my hand. Finally, I smiled and asked you to HU for a half hour so you could settle your energy to understand the effects it can produce.

"People's energy can actually control the weather, and their energy controls circumstances in their lives. That is why we want to live with a quiet mind. Living with a quiet mind is when we are interacting within the environment as Soul, or things manifest as we are doing them. Therefore, we do not have sparks of chaos to go with it.

"When you live with a chattering mind, you can create all kinds of problems. Suddenly, things may start to spark up in people while you are talking to them. If they are not living as Soul, they might suddenly get very irritated, or uneasy. Even if they are living as Soul, they will feel uneasy in your presence. They may even snap at you.

"All of these things exist because your energy is frazzled. Yes, let's say frazzled. Frazzled is a very good word for it, because you are internalizing all of these pictures of things that need to be done. In your exterior world, you are moving that energy from the pictures of your internal world to the outside and it has nothing to do with the present moment. That is why we live in the present moment. Your actions should match what is going on in your mind. It is very important to match the pictures in your mind with your actions. Does that make sense to you?"

Leaping Deer: "Yes, it does."

"The best thing you can do for yourself when you are like that is to take a nap. If you cannot get back as Soul, lie down and take a nap. Stay still. At least, get out of other people's space, and get out of your own space.
    "If your attention conflicts with your actions, you are going to have all kinds of sparks. Picking up the vitamin capsules was a perfect example, that is, each time I picked up a capsule, it flew out of my hand."

Leaping Deer: "It does that for me at work too."

"Yes, and it is your responsibility to not let it happen. That is chaotic power. That is what people would call poltergeist action. It is not an entity outside of yourself, these are your own entities that you carry within yourself. Do you see? It is scattered energy, and that is what poltergeist action is, scattered energy."

Leaping Deer: "So does it mean I am not in the present moment?"

"That's right. You are not in the present moment.
    "Pay very close attention. As you are sitting here, can you feel your skin? Feel the skin on your leg, the skin on your chest, the skin on your back, the skin on the top of your head, the skin on the end of your nose, the skin on

your cheeks, the skin on our hands and your fingers. *Feel* the skin on your body. *FEEL* the skin on your body. Now that you can feel it, feel the blood flow inside of the skin. What you are feeling is your own energy that flows through your body in the bloodstream.

"The energy that is flowing through your bloodstream is controlled by muscle reactions. You can speed it up or slow it down, because it is controlled by nerves. The muscles and nerves work together. Now, again, feel that blood flow next to your skin. FEEL IT. It is a little tingling feeling, a little pressure feeling. That is the way you live with the energy contained right up at the skin.

"Now, if you feel that your energy is pushing out at some point, you are leaking, and when you leak, you create chaos. *Don't do that!* Persons of power always live with their energy pushed up against their skin. Be a person of power, that way, when you reach your hand out to do something, all of the strength that is needed from the energy goes right to what you are doing. This is because your mind then, is in line with your energy. When your mind is aligned with every movement of your body, your energy is directly at your command. That is something that you have to consciously work on."

*Standing Turtle: "Could you give an example of how to pull the energy in?"*

"All right. Sit down cross-legged like you were going to HU. If you can sit cross legged, it is better than sitting in a chair, but if you have to sit in a chair, that is okay, but I want you to be at attention. It is important to be at attention and to have your spine straight. It is important not to be slouched back, so if you need to loosen clothing, do it. Sit forward and find that pivot position. Put your hands on your knees. The reason you put your hands on your knees is so that nothing is cutting off the blood flow, the energy flow in your body while you are sitting. Notice that your chest is wide open, so you can breathe.

"Sit up straight. Take in a breath. (Winged Wolf demonstrates by breathing deeply through the nose with the breath coming in at the back of the throat). As you do that, become conscious of the air that is going into your body. Feel that.

"Now as you exhale into the HU, be aware that you are pushing that energy flow up against your skin. When you are taking air in, you are pulling your energy in. (Demonstrates by breathing deeply) Then the energy is pushed up against your skin, HUUUUUUUUUUUUUUUUUUUUU. You have to try it. (Winged Wolf demonstrates with each apprentice, HUUUUUUUUUUUUUUUUUUUUUUUUUUUUU."

*Leaping Deer: "I can feel it in back of my hands."*

"Okay, but you do not let it flow out. Just feel it. Contain it. Contain that energy! Now, sit still. Can you feel that energy up around your skin? Can you feel it on your legs? Can you feel it on the top of your head? (To Standing Turtle) You are scratching your head. Are you not quite sure?"

*Standing Turtle: "It was itching all of a sudden."*

"Good. The energy is going to the top of your head. Feel it in your arms. It is easy to feel it in your cheeks, it just rises right up. You do that as you are HUing. So, become aware of the energy rising in your body.

"You do not want to fill up a room with your energy, you want to keep that energy contained. This is your capsule. Now, I have spoken before about a capsule being a few inches from the body. I think that is too hard for you in the beginning, so just use your body, itself, as the capsule. Your body is filled with this energy and the energy is not able to come out.

"The more you HU and do it that way, you will build energy in your body and you will be like a beacon of light when you walk out, because you are centered. You are enlivened as Soul, but your mind has to be still. Will you work on that?"

Leaping Deer: "I sure will."

"Good. It will be an interesting experience to see what it gives you. I promise you this, HUing this way will greatly enhance your life. It will make you a person of power. When your mind is quiet, your energy flow is contained and everything that you reach out to do, will manifest very quickly."

*"When you live with a chattering mind, you can create all kinds of problems. Suddenly, things may start to spark up in people while you are talking to them. If they are not living as Soul, they might suddenly get very irritated, or uneasy."*

# CONTAINING ENERGY

**Winged Wolf:** "May the blessings be.

"I would like to talk about containing energy. When you have somebody on your mind, or you have been looking at them in your mind's eye over a period of time, that means they are looking at you, and whatever feeling it is that you are getting about them, is the feeling being projected by them towards you. Now, if there is something you need to take care of, do it. The wisest and easiest way of defusing energy, if it is long distance, is to pick up the phone and talk to the person, or sit down and write them a letter. Do something in answer to that energy that is coming at you.

"If you cannot do any of those things, for whatever reason, and you feel you need to have resolution to the feeling, do <u>not</u> envision them or go through telepathic silliness. Instead, formulate an answer to the feeling that is comfortable for you to accept. When you do that, dismiss it and put your attention on the Third Eye.

"When you have an uncomfortable feeling, because you have a particular focus toward someone and it is *your* focus, the best way to handle it is not to focus your energy on that person. This is because you are getting into somebody else's space. The more intense your feeling, the more intensely you are getting into their space. That is what we call oozing."

*Leaping Deer: "Is that manipulating?"*

"Yes, your feelings would manipulate the energy of the other person. It is like you were sitting there and listening to them tell you about their feelings and vice versa, so,

63

you are getting in their psychic space. When you do that, there is a penalty.

"The penalty: You make a karmic bond with that person and that karmic bond begins to grow roots, so the roots get deeper and deeper and deeper. Now, the roots are not necessarily something you want, or do not want. They will not grow as you intend them, because the other half of those roots are connected to the other person. There is an enmeshment between the two of you. It is intention that pushes the roots deeper. When the other person comes in contact with energy you are putting out, the two together form a karmic bond. You might have intended one thing; but, because of your intensity, it is received as another. Your intensity mixes with the nature of the other person and their myth. The two put together is what is being received and that is the karmic bond.

"So, if you are looking at a problem with a child of yours, say with a daughter, your daughter feels this energy, but she receives it as an interference from you. Your karmic roots get intertwined in a way that you did not intend, because of the coming together of your energy and your daughters.

"Eventually these things will work out; but, it is best to leave them alone. This is why we say it is not wise to send loving energy to anyone, anymore than it is to send unpleasant energy, because when you are sending loving energy to someone, they might interpret it as interference, or it might come across very negatively. All you can do is, release your feeling and let it go with no intensity.

"Containing energy has many facets to it. I know we have talked about the energy capsule but there is much, much more you need to understand in order to be effective in that capsule, otherwise, you will be resistant."

# LIGHT & DARK

**Winged Wolf:** "Where there is darkness there is light, and where there is light there is darkness. In the physical world there is always a contrast. In deep darkness there is always light, because deep darkness is light turned inward. Deep darkness exists because the light has become so intense, it turns upon itself and becomes dark, pitch, pitch black.

"In other words, true darkness contains all light, so to say that dark and light are separate, is not correct. One cannot exist without the other. Where there is form, there is shadow, form being the light and shadow being intense light of the form, or the intense light projected from the form.

"Shadow is projection of light hitting the form, and mirrored on top of other matter, you see, whether it be on the grass, on the ground, against a tree, or against the plastic windows in the Happy House.

"Light, itself, comes from the Void in its bright form, as well as its dark form. Actually, it comes out of the dark form. Out of the Void comes complete darkness. As energy moves and manifests itself, it takes on light. Without the light, energy could not be manifested. It could not grow, it could not appear. So, dark objects appear when there is light.

"Without going into the story of creation, which we have done on other occasions, people have an opportunity to make use of the light and the dark, without manipulaton, through observation of it.

"Now, both of you told me a few minutes ago how you observed lights last night. (Speaking to Gazelle and Ravenwolf). What you saw might have been the light of the moon coming through the windows, or through a crack in the door. Even if this is so, it does not take away from your experience. So don't say, 'Oh, well, that's the light of the moon, that's nothing.' What is the light of the moon? The moon is darkness in its darkest form. As it manifests, it becomes light. You saw something becoming manifest, something appearing.

"There is no difference between seeing the light of the moon and so-called phenomena. You see, everything is all the same. When people say, 'it could have been my imagination', what is imagination, except darkness with light shed on it? Imagination is little sparkles of light in images and form. It is nothing more than a pure dark screen like everything else is a pure dark screen, until there is movement and energy put to it. The energy produces light, and then you have the appearance of form. That is what you saw here in the Happy House. You saw an appearance of form. The appearance of form, in this case, was caused by all the activity in the Happy House, during the process of it being drywalled by people who are trying to do a good job, doing something they have never done before. There is much energy left behind and it shows up in the darkness through little streaks and sparks.

"Energy sparksoccur within a human being, as well. When a human being becomes engrossed in the darkness of themselves, they turn inward. Something will disturb them and energy will spark. Sparks of light will come out of them, through their movements, through their sorrow, their anger. Do you see? Strong feeling is projected.

"When someone is angry, their anger is like a dark oozing matter, a dark murky red color oozing out of that person. The murky red is murky because it actually has little puss spots in it. It is quite ugly, ugly in that you can feel a distortion of the clarity of dark and light. The energy is conjured, a manipulaed energy that has a fierce expression as it pushes outward. As it pushes outward, sparks fly, but the light that comes with it is an impure light.

"Every emotion and every feeling comes from darkness within the body and projects outward as light. Each emotion exhibits a hue of color to indicate intensification, according to what is being felt.

"Now, here is where we get into part of what you experienced. There were confused images projected into the environment, forms that became visible in the darkness. They were energy sparks, not necessarily anger, or grief, or anything of that sort, but anxiety, and anxiety has a way of propelling energy. It has its own kind of relationship. It has a color to it as well.

"All feelings produce color. The color is produced by the intensity of the light and the dark. When artists sit down to paint, they mix their colors and, as they mix their colors, they come from dark into light. That is the way it works for us, as well, when we have striking thoughts of any kind. The color images are actually produced from the intensity we are feeling inside of ourselves.

"The most destructive of these, because it has an intense deep, murky, sickness to it, is anger. Religions that specialize on the dark side, like Voo Doo, actually conjure up anger inside themselves. Some American Indian Tribes used to do that when they were doing a war dance. You conjure up anger against your enemies, and that anger produces an ugly front that proceeds you as you approach. Anger manipulates energy.

"So, all emotions project images. As people walk into these images, they can feel the energy left behind. For instance, as you walk into a room, you can feel various types of energy. It may feel really good or it may feel like you have to get the heck out of there. The feeling that you have to 'get out', may be caused by anger images left behind. If you were really aware, prepared to see what was going on, you could notice sparks of color left behind

67

by these images. But most of the time, you walk into a room and you are hurried and you do not see the sparks, but you see a fleeting color on the floor, in people's clothing, and on the ceiling. You may see little shadows on the ceiling, very subtle shadows, the color in them. Begin to be observant of your surroundings, not through thinking so much or analyzing, but through observation and recognition.

"When you walk into a place and certain imagery strikes you - attracts or repels you - recognize it. People can directly project a feeling at you and, if you are not on your toes, it can actually knock you over or even affect your health. Husbands and wives murder each other all the time. I mean literally murder, not through hitting each other or poisoning each other; but, nevertheless, it is poison in a sense. You see, what they do is, they think ugly things about the other person. Gradually, the other person's confidence begins to wane. You can see one person suddenly loses a lot of weight, while the other person puts it on. The energy is being imbalanced and used like that.

"Perhaps somebody feels timid because their spouse is always thinking how stupid they are and how dependent they are on them. What would they do without them, and this, that, and the other thing. Even though the spouse did not say it aloud, their emotional imagery projects to the other person and that other person then begins to act out what is being thought about them.

"So, there is much going on that is not verbalized or visually seen that you can be aware of, by the energy you perceive. This is very important to one who wants to become a Spiritual Warrior. You are responsible for everything you think and, if you feel for an instant that no one will know about it, you are wrong. They will know. Maybe they are not aware that they know, but they will sense something about you that is disturbing to them. The further along you go on the spiritual scale, the more you recognize energy and where it is coming from. As you move along the Path of Soul you will begin to discriminate where you allow yourself to be, and with whom, because of the energy they project in your space.

"Love and hate in the dual worlds are addictions. I do not want any apprentices to be addicted to me. I want my apprentices to stand strong on their own two feet, to one day become Shaman themselves.

"Light and dark: Get to know the light inside of yourself and transmit it to that which you want to propagate. Live the beauty of yourself. Have many, many, many pretty pictures in your mind. Look at things that are beautiful. Do not look at things that are ugly, or if you look at something that was once ugly, find the beauty in it. If there are maggots in a trash can and it is ugly to you, do not look at it. If you feel you can find something beautiful in that; well, go ahead and look. That is your choice, do you see? But, don't look at things simply to test yourself; to force yourself to look at something because you think you should. Accept the images that are naturally beautiful.

"When somebody has a preference to live comfortably, there is nothing wrong with that. It is wonderful to live comfortably as long as you are not so obsessed with comfort that you think you will be miserable without it. Be flexible, yet discriminate. Get to know the light and the dark forces inside of you, darkness not being bad or negative, but just being the opposite of light. Sometimes to sit in the darkness is like sitting in a cave. You can sit in total darkness and, when you become accustomed to that darkness, you will see that it is really light.

"I spent seven days in a cave one time. It was totally dark. At first, the darkness was very disturbing, hauntingly disturbing. You could not even see your hand in front of your face. Then, just like being in a foreign country and not being able to speak the language, you begin to understand the darkness. You begin to understand the energy that is there. You begin to see that the darkness is not really darkness at all, it really has light to it because, you are feeling that energy. And as you are watching the flow and feeling the flow of energy, you begin to actually see the energy. It gets quite exciting.

"So, to take a stand and say that darkness is one thing and light is another, means you have not yet really experienced both.

"Learn to live without emotion. Learn to live with feeling instead of emotion. Emotion is nothing more than regurgitated mind stuff, rebellious sensations about dead images that compare the past with the present. Feeling, on the other hand, is a gift from Soul. It is intuition, or Soul speaking through the body as feeling.

"Real Love is not an emotion. There is a love that is an emotion. That type of love, while it may be passionate when you are twenty, is total insanity. It is a mental passion, which consumes you. You actually lose control of your world when you are "in love". That type of love is obsessive. Divine love is freedom enlivened from Soul.

"Leave anger alone. Anger is the ugliest of emotions. If you lose loved ones, grieve and let go of them. It is natural to miss people that you love, but after you have missed them for a time, let go of them.

"Learn the art of 'having without attachment'. Be happy, but be happy beyond duality. Leave pleasure for pleasure's sake alone, because sure enough, as soon as you get caught in pleasure, there is a flip side to it, and that is pain. Pleasure is an emotion. Learn joy instead. Joy is not an emotion. Joy is a gift of spirit. It is a balancing factor. It is when the light and darkness merge within you absolutely."

*Two Eagles: "How do you transmute energy? Anger in particular."*

"When you are angry, it is fruitless to try to be centered at the Third Eye, because you are imbalanced by your anger and it takes a bit of balance to center at the Third Eye. What I would suggest at this point, is to go outside, into your backyard and part the grass with your fingers. Put your face down into that parting of the grass. Actually, rub your face in the dirt. I want you to smell the Earth. If you have something ugly to say, say it with your face in the dirt. Let the dirt absorb it. It does not like it either, but it will transmute that energy.

"A spiritual teacher can transmute your negative energy, also. However, the difficulty is, you will make the teacher sick, because a teacher does not reflect anything back to you, unless the connection between you and your teacher is severed, at which point, your anger is then mirrored back to you.

"The best way to deal with your negative energy is to *never* expose it to another person. If you are at work, and you cannot go out and put your face on the ground, walk into a closet, take a piece of cardboard, rip it off of a box and wrap that piece of cardboard up close to your face. Better yet, if you are an angry person, and you are perpetually losing your temper, get a plastic bag full of dirt. If it is wintertime where you live, and the ground is frozen, so go to a garden shop and buy a bag of top soil. Carry a plastic bag full of dirt or soil with you to work. Put your face into it whenever you are angry. If you are going to do that, you may need to carry some handi-wipes to clean your face afterwards. (Laughs). Chances are, you will begin laughing at yourself and that energy will be transmuted.

"Of course, the first thing you want to do, as soon as you get back into balance again, is to focus at the

71

Third Eye, because that is what sustains balance and health. It is the place where you communicate with other people, to get the return that you want, not in a manipulative way, but in a very natural way. So, get your baggies out! If you are suddenly angry at somebody, make a dash for the bathroom, or just open up that baggie. Who cares what anybody thinks? Stick your face into that dirt. I mean stick your nose right in it!

"If your wife makes you angry or your husband makes you angry, it is not their fault. You are the one who is angry. I know this is a tough one to swallow. This does not mean that your spouse does not have to work with you at some point, but they cannot work with you when you are angry. Anger destructs a marriage. *Stop it!*

*Two Eagles: "Is it true to say that anything but joy is some expression of anger?'*

"So what does that mean to you? It means that if you have a problem with anger, you decide whether or not you want to deal with it. Do you want anger in your life? Do you feel that it is a natural part of your life? Do you need to use it to express yourself? That is your decision. It is your right and prerogative to have what you want in your life, but you may not bring it into my life unless I agree, do you see?

"I will work with you as long as you are doing your part, but you are not doing your part as long as you are throwing anger at someone, or if you are throwing anger at me. Just because I am your teacher does not give you the right to take a hammer to me.

"If you resent authority figures, that is too bad. Life is filled with authority figures. Most likely you are an authority figure yourself to some people at work or with your families. Get accustomed to it. It is time for the 'little self' to go. It is time for freedom, if that is what you choose, freedom from anger! Use the little baggie of dirt. I am really serious about doing this.

"The same subject comes up so many times with complaints about work, 'Well, there is this problem with the bureaucracy, and that problem with the bureaucracy.' Always remember, when you made a choice to accept your job, you made an agreement to do it your employer's way. You have nothing to be angry about. If you don't like it, leave.

"Make conscious choices and be responsible for the choices you make. Accept the choices you make. Do your best, 100 percent, not 95 percent. Don't say, 'Well, I work for a bureaucracy, so I will only give them 70 percent'. *No.* That is not walking the Path of Soul. Do your best, 100 percent. While you are at work, become ONE with your job. Whatever it takes, give it.

"If you decide to marry, give 100% to your marriage. If you are unhappy with your marriage, then leave it. That is your choice, but do not do anything half heartedly, because you are not living as Soul.

"Light and dark: Where is the balance in your life? All life is integrated, the dark into light and the light into dark. The point of integration comes from wholeheartedness. It comes when you impeccably give all of yourself, to whatever it is that you are doing in the moment. That is the point of integration, when you become ONE with that, whatever it is.

"If you are driving the car, drive the car. If you are cooking dinner, cook dinner. Make the meal the best you can. People can then really enjoy it. The tensions of their day melt away, because what is put before them was done wholeheartedly with love. You do not have to think about putting love into the food. If you are giving yourself to the moment, you are love. Do you see? Do not conjure things. That is manipulation. That is like witchcraft. Leave that alone.

"Don't try to be spiritual. Be spiritual by being ONE with life, being ONE with the moment. That is where the light and dark are integrated, one to the other, and it is through this balance of integrating one to the other that manifestation occurs. That is how you present your life. Do you see? You Present your life through being integrated with the light and the dark, through balance of the two, by drawing on the light or by drawing on the dark. Again, darkness does not mean being negative and light does not mean being positive, because they are the same force. They are One."

# NOT GETTING CAUGHT UP IN ANOTHER'S STUFF

**Winged Wolf:** "We are going to be talking about companion energy and not getting caught up in other people's stuff, their situations and karma, yet getting mixed up in their stuff in order to have companion energy.

"When two people are working together, one puts out a hand to do this and the other may use the same hand to do the same thing. If they are in movement together, then one hand will touch the object, and the other hand will touch the object, and the object will be lifted by the two, and it will seem like nothing. At this point, usually a smile passes from one face to another and someone says, 'Oh, how light it is. How easy that task was'. The execution of it was nothing because it was in companion energy. Do you see?

"Now, if one person reaches for something, putting a hand on it, and the other person puts a hand on it and says, 'I'll take care of that', then there is opposition. The person who takes care of that actually has an empowered feeling perhaps for a split second because he took the weight. But, if the individual that started to work with it has some mind chatter about, 'Well, I could have done that, blah, blah, blah', instantly, the energy is split and the next action goes down hill. And the action after that goes down hill even more.

"So, companion energy is a movement of things together. In that same situation, it could be a release of one person too, who would say, 'Oh, that is great that you want to do that. Here, you do it', but, that has to be comfortable, you see? It has to always be all right. It is good to do that as long as there is a release. But very

75

often, that is not the case; what happens is the case is the other person's mind will hang on to it and think about it while the person who took the responsibility will come back and say, 'Well, what is wrong with you?' Well, what is wrong with you is, you started to do something and got cut off and did not release it. It is not that it was your responsibility to release it anymore than it was the other person's responsibility to take control of the situation. As a spiritual warrior, it is to your benefit to release it. Go ahead. If they want to carry the burden, let them do it. Simply drop it with no attitude about it. Just let go. Release.

"Now, real companion energy is that upliftment of whatever it is that is being done, because it becomes very simple and very easy through this movement of the flow. Remember after 'The Gathering', when everybody was of one mind, one consciousness, after being together for one week, they went to clean up and it was swiftly done without any large discussion or question of any kind. It was just harmonious and easy. This is the same principle.

"When you start taking on other people's stuff and do not work in unison, it compounds and creates an odd cycle of karma where you actually are taking on the other individual's mind-set. Because you did not go with the flow and you did not release your own choice to their choice, what happens is, you are at odds. And at odds means, you begin to take on the aspects of the other person's personality because you are irritated by them. Do you see? Anything you are irritated by, you begin to act out yourself in opposite form. In doing that, you are opposing and conflicting. So, a cycle is now set in motion that is going around full circle. It can be interrupted, if you know how to do it. Rather than live out the cycle to full circle by saying nothing and occasionally reflecting back, which perpetuates the cycle with little bits and pieces added to it, simply acknowledge the fact that a cycle is in motion to yourself, and the next time a different piece of that cycle presents itself, you simply say, 'Release' to yourself and *let go.*

"Now, it will come back. Little situations from that situation come back in odd little ways throughout your life because that cycle is put in motion, unless it is interrupted. The hardest thing is to catch it the very first time. After you catch it the first time, the second time is easier. After you catch it the second time, it's a piece of cake, *you've interrupted the cycle!*

"When you interrupt the cycle, there is no real going back to it because you will spot it every time it comes up and you will just drop it. And maybe, one day your partner or friend will also spot that cycle because they will have nothing to hang on to. Do you see? When there is no irritation to continue it, the cycle stops, and maybe the other person too, will reflect and see that it disappears.

"It doesn't matter how it disappears. There is no reason to talk about it, because to talk about it, is to drag it up. To be interested in it yourself might be very useful because, as you begin to get yourself in a similar situation, you will spot it and say, 'No, I don't want to do that this time.' If you have broken a cycle once with one situation, you will get so you will break the cycle before it begins or before it develops into a cycle the next time. Soon, you will catch it even before it gets going the time after that. So, it is your choice. You have to make these conscious choices to say, 'I want to get into this or I don't want to get into this.'

"Now, another aspect of this is the unspoken mind stuff. For instance, yesterday I could feel my mother pulling at me from the mainland. I also knew she was lonely and wanted to see me. Well, I had a business meeting along with other chores in the morning. Looking at the clock and then the ferry time schedule, I said to Standing Turtle that I would be going on the 1:40 p.m. ferry to the mainland.

Now after I said it, it occurred to me that I did not say it out loud to her, not that it mattered, because she felt it or knew it anyway.

"So many times, when you get an impulse that has no real meaning to you, or you feel no real purpose for having that impulse, check yourself out. 'Why do I feel this way? What is occurring to cause this feeling? Nothing is going on, I have no reason to feel this way.' Do you see? If you get that answer, then STOP. Pull your energy back into yourself. Your energy is extended and connected in a bold way to another person. Now maybe, you do not know right away who that person is, so pull your energy into yourself. Get your energy inside your skin, pressed up tightly against your skin, and then go about your business. Next, take notice of images that flash in your mind. Occasionally, there may be a subtle image of a person passing through on your mental screen. Even if unclear, the image passing through may give you a clue as to where that feeling came from. Then you have a choice. You can either ask the person what is going on, or you could play scientist and sit back and wait. Do you see? You could sit back, wait, and say, 'Well, I'm going to see what is going on here.' Maybe it is something you would not feel comfortable mentioning at that time because it feels like it would just be so much out of context, like you are dreaming something up' that is not really in sync with somebody else; then, you just wait and see. You will get an answer in short notice that is equivalent to the timing of what is taking place. Once you come into contact with the reason, the wisest thing to do, since it was not your stuff to begin with, is to say, 'Ho, ho, that's what it was', and let it go.

"Go about your business as a grounded being, not like the wind that is constantly trying to get in somewhere as it is in this building. (The wind bangs against the sides of the Happy House). The wind is saying, 'I want to come in, I want

78

to come in.' The wind is an astral force. It does not like to be withheld. It does not meet true resistance with this building, because instead of glass, there is plastic, which flaps when it hits it. The plastic pops up and back. The wind gives the impression that it feels like it should be able to go through. It moves by instinct and force.

"The wind moves by attraction and repulsion, and that is the way people move. In instinctual form, people are propelled and repelled into motion. When you have an urge to do something, you're like the wind. That astral part of you is coming in contact with something else and it starts to move and is propelled forward. Other times, when it comes in contact with something, it will be repelled and will go back. Or it will come up to someone in an attraction way, and that which it is attracted to, will have a force around it that repels you, or makes you keep pushing forward. It is like a suitor in pursuit of a woman, or a woman in pursuit of a man. There will be that, 'I'm not interested', but then the suitor keeps going forward until eventually, the wall comes down. So the male part of a human being, though it is contained within the female as well, is more adept at perseverance, because perseverance is a male trait.

"People who live strongly in the opposite, or the female part of a human being, have to learn perseverance. So, all these things have to do with your interactions with other people, and you become more and more aware of it as you interact. If you feel someone constantly approaching and you do not want to get involved for whatever reason, simply do not resist. Keep your barrier, your boundary steady. That is all. Nothing can penetrate it.

"Now, the unfortunate part of that perseverant energy, if it is developed in a human being, is that it never gives up. And interestingly enough, it does penetrate the most impenetrable wall. In some way, and maybe not in the way it is trying to reach, the wind certainly makes noise even though it cannot come in, and its noise attracts attention, so in a sense the wind is making a statement, even though it did not come in.

"People make statements to each other all the time. Be alert to those statements. Start paying attention-- have conscious, not unconscious attention. Know what statements are being made, not to have a judgment, but just for awareness sake, not to mull over and think about so much as just to be aware, just to be conscious. It makes life very interesting.

"As you become more aware of the energies around you, it is important that you do not interfere in any way, because if you do, you are game playing, which turns into manipulation. Simply observe. Act out what you want to act out, and let the other individuals do what they have to do."

*Two Eagles: "That's a big one."*

"It is a big one. Why is it a big one?"

*Two Eagles: "Well, the temptation in my awareness, especially if I may not like what I am aware of, is that I may want to change it and make it different. And, if I do like it, I may want more of it and try to magnify it."*

"Well, you can magnify it just through your attention, but you do not have to try to magnify it. You simply acknowledge what is there and it is magnified. There is nothing to do about it, do you see? It is when you think that you have something to do about it that you get into trouble. I know this is an entirely different concept from the way you were taught living in the world. This is a hands off approach and yet it is totally your choice and decision every step of the way, but there is no manipulation involved in it."

*Wings of Change: There is really nothing wrong with saying, 'Oh, I want more of that?"*

"No, those are just words, but it is striking an intent, isn't it? It is not necessary because, what attracts you should be that which you want in your life. Now, to most people that rule cannot apply. We are speaking of living as Soul. For people who do not live as Soul, that which attracts them is not necessarily what they want in their life. They are attracted by horror shows and murder news on TV, and blood and gore, and they don't particularly want that in their lives. But as Soul, that which attracts, automatically becomes. It also *becomes* for the person who is not as Soul, but they don't know it. The person who lives as Soul does not pay any attention to things like that. There is no point in living with your head in a garbage can.

"Who wants to be reminded of garbage? One of these days everybody will catch on and not do it. Do you see? The mind should be filled full of beautiful pictures.

"Do not look at anything that is ugly. Now, I realize ugly is relative, because as Soul, ugly can be beautiful. However, this does not mean that gore is beautiful. Use selective perception, and selective attention. As Soul, look at beautiful scenery. Look at a smile on someone's face. Enjoy the laughter of the moment in a scene of people in a belly laugh together. Enjoy a happy voice on the telephone. Enjoy watching a horse run across a field, and the geese going out on the pond. This is a beautiful setting because I want to look at pretty things. I want pretty things in my mind. I do not care to have ugliness in my mind, or horror shows in my mind. I am very careful what I look at.

"I like going to the post office here in this charming little seaport village. It has a postmaster who smiles a lot. After we got through the adjustment period, the postmaster smiled a lot. See? This does not mean that sometimes you do not have to go through little adjustment periods to

81

transmute the energy that is there. You do. The old energy has to become accustomed to the new energy. The new energy coming in, either adds to or detracts. If I bring a smile into the post office that is natural and warm, well it is going to put a smile on somebody's face that is natural and warm."

*Wings of Change: "A question comes up in our study group often when we are talking about this subject of not putting our head in the garbage pail. Many people say that that is living in a state of denial or unawareness. You cannot go through life not looking at the negative side. You cannot ignore all the pain, suffering, and poverty, etc. Specifically, two women in our group that have been sexually molested, had a big response about, 'Well, you have to be aware of these things. I was just walking down the street and I was thinking everything was wonderful, and suddenly I got raped. I can't go around in life like that.' How would you address or respond to that type of comment?"*

"People who feel they have to be aware of the negative side of life, or the negative actions of other people, are stuck in a paradoxical world, the world of duality that says, 'This is this on one side and this is that on the other side'.

"One who lives as Soul has been there; and therefore, carries great compassion for those individuals, but I say to you, it does not have to be that way. As long as someone is trapped in the paradoxical world, it will have to be that way for them. Living as Soul, there is a choice, a conscious choice to see the beauty of life. *Life is beautiful.* If you are seeing the beauty as Soul, not as fantasy within the mind, that is the difference. If someone, who is trapped in the paradoxical world says, 'I create a fantasy and live in that', then they are trapped in the paradoxical world and their fantasies will be constantly bombarded with negative images. Their attention will wander to horror scenes. Their fears will pull their attention

82

to what they do not want, do you see? As long as there is fear, you are trapped in the paradoxical world.

"Now, beyond fear, one lives as Soul. Once you can do that, something happens. No longer does that which you were afraid of, come to you. You do not end up the person who is raped, robbed, or beaten, or the person without anything. As Soul, the individual is very, very grounded. Everything is solid. Now, that is not to say that you do not have difficulties that you have to deal with from time to time. No human can live in the God worlds one hundred percent of the time, but ninety percent, yes!

"Beyond ninety percent of living in the God worlds as Soul, you really cannot live in a physical body, or if you live in a physical body, you would have to live quietly secluded, totally withdrawn."

*Wings of Change: "Can you say why that is?"*

"The world would be too abrasive. Abrasiveness is being around anger. The further you go on the path, the more difficult it is for you to be around anger. Anger has a devastating effect on the body, and the further you go, because of your own awareness, when you come in contact with anger, it whacks you all over the place. It is like somebody taking a baseball bat and swinging it wildly at you.

"It does that to people who are not living as Soul, as well, only they are not aware of it because they are toughened by everything else that goes on. If you are living as Soul, you are very susceptible. You are very vulnerable, so you begin to pull away from that. You get a little smarter as you go along, and you live quietly."

*Standing Turtle: "When we are living somewhere, we interact with other people."*

"People need to interact until they reach the point of really living as Soul. That does not mean that one living as Soul is alone, but they have no more need of doing that. You see, you have that great need of interacting because that is how you learn. That is how you experience life, but that is not life. That is the learning of how life operates. I can tell you that interacting with people for the sake of interacting with people to learn, is not life in its purest form. The enjoyment of that, of being with someone of like-consciousness, or like-mind, is certainly wonderful, but you no longer are dependent upon another person.

"That feeling that you get sometimes of almost panic, of giving up who you were, is a very natural feeling as you move along the path. As you get closer and closer to giving it up, at first it strikes almost like panic inside of you, 'What will happen to me? What will I be like?' It is like falling off the edge of a cliff. It is letting go. But, once you pass that, you are no longer bound to the world, yet you can have and participate in what you want of the world. You 'become'.

"Do you remember at the end of the movie, *Groundhog Day*, where Phil suddenly became a part of the world that he really liked? Well, that is the way it is. You see, the world then responds the same to you. There is no more friction, or very little. And, if people do experience friction with you, it does not do anything because they have no place to hook it. There is no argument, so you live freely."

*Wings of Change: "Does the fear of letting go come from some mental-set that says there is danger somehow?"*

"No, it comes from some mental-set that says, 'You don't know what's there.' So, it is a fear of danger, a fear of the unknown. You do not know what is out there. I will tell you, quite frankly, that I have no idea; but I can see a short distance ahead. Other than that, it is pure darkness but I am always walking toward the darkness. Never forget, darkness is intense light, and I am not afraid of it anymore. Sometimes my body still trembles involuntarily, but it is from the vibration of the unknown Itself, the vibration of the Void. It is not fear."

*Standing Turtle: "So you can continue living in the city, walking down the street, without having that fear that somebody is going to jump out at an unexpected moment, because your body senses what is there and the safety of it? And if it was not safe, you wouldn't be there?"*

"I cannot say this for sure, but I would say this from the point of view where I stand, and from the point of view where my teacher stood and my teacher's teachers, and of others that are also on this path that I do not know personally, that I do not think you would find a spiritual adept living in the city. I am not saying that they would never visit the city. One of the main reasons is the mind chatter in the city. Even if you do not listen to it, it is in constant noise like a radio turned on full blast. It is not a pretty picture. The pretty picture is being closer to the Earth."

*Standing Turtle: "I was still trying to line up with the woman that spoke of all the stuff going on. I would still walk down the street. I do not have any fear."*

"That is right, because you do not look at the ugly images of rape and crime. And as long as you do not look at those images, then they are not lodged in your brain, ready to jump out at you. What you carry in your brain, attracts. It is like a beacon. Of course, the argument comes, 'Well, when I was a little girl, was I a beacon?" It is  karmic when things happen to a child. It happens because somehow, I am sorry to say, they brought on the

85

misfortune through something they did in a past life. It is horrible and unfortunate, but it is true. We come into life with circumstances that we earned from the past.

"I wish that it could be easily changed for people but they are here to work through that, so rather than get angry and upset about it, say, 'That was then, but from now on I am going to break that cycle.' And, that cycle can be broken by learning to center yourself at the Third Eye. It is just that simple, not easy, but simple. It is not easy because of the myth that has been perpetuated. The myth are those fantasies that have to be broken to make it possible for you to live at the Third Eye. You have to be clear to live there.

"People have to be conscious and they have to be willing to let go of their anger and be willing to let go of their fear and victimization. People get attached. They are angry. 'This is mine, don't try to touch it.' Well, they will come back, born again and again, until they let go.

*Two Eagles: "Does the holding on to it continually increase the karma?*

"Well, the longer you do something, the more of a habit it becomes. You begin to spin more of a tale, don't you? The spider web grows. The spider web grows just to keep this little piece alive here, to keep it safe and separated from everything else. It is all a fantasy! Everything that is woven around the incident is a fantasy, but it keeps the karma nurtured and alive. It is the very thing that the person does not want becomes bigger and greater. So, you need to have a teacher to wipe that thing away and say, 'Look, this is what we are looking at -- not all this, let's just remove this.' And they say, 'Oh No, I've got to have that. What are we going to do without that?' that is why people strike out at the teacher. They are angry and say, 'You are taking that. It's mine."

*Wings of Change: "So, one must have a teacher to achieve Soul Consciousness?"*

"Absolutely. There is no other way. I never could have made it without Alana. It can't be done alone, because you get caught up in your own boxes."

*Wings of Change: "I think that is real important for people to understand that at some point, they must have a teacher."*

*Standing Turtle: "Without a teacher we are seeing nothing but what the brain has sent to fantasize with. You can't get past your own mind."*

"That's right. But be careful when you accept a teacher. Know something about that person. Watch them. Be with them awhile. Don't just run in and give yourself. There are people who call themselves teachers, who never were students. Now, if you cannot be the apprentice, then you cannot be the teacher. The teacher is one who truly learned to be the apprentice. Do you see? It is the same principle that, in order to lead, you have to know what following is about. So, take your time. People can go to functions where that teacher is, or where their students are. That is what the study groups are about. People can come in, sit down and hear about the teachings, and be with students of the teacher. They can see what it has done for them and how they are. It is the same principle as, if you want to know something about adults, you hang around their children. The children will tell you everything."

*Standing Turtle: "From their viewpoint though."*

"The students will tell you everything from their viewpoint, by their behavior and their demeanor. The energy that flows from their demeanor will tell you about them. You will catch their link with the teacher. If you like what you see, then seek out the teacher. Although you may have to wait until you are prepared. The teacher might hold you at a distance a little bit. You may have to work off some of the garbage before you are allowed to come close. Go take a bath first. You have been out there sweating in your karma for umpteen million years and you want to bring it in. Well, you might be asked to do some things out there first, lovingly, because the teacher has been there too, and the teacher understands at that point why h/his teacher didn't want new students close. So, the teacher knows where you are coming from."

Wings of Change: "They don't know about being covered in sweat."

"No. I never believed Alana did not want me around. How could she not want me around? I was so intelligent, and wonderful, and charming. (Laughs) I must have lit up her life. Sometimes I would go up into the mountains and I would never find her. I would think, 'Well, isn't that odd, she doesn't know I'm here.' HA! She knew I was there."

Wings of Change: "She was avoiding you?"

"Yes, she was. Sometimes I would stay and wait for weeks. I would say to myself, 'surely I will bump into her somewhere', then I would go out looking for her. She might be hiding behind a tree, I didn't know. But I never saw her at those times, and here I had traveled hundreds of miles. It cost a lot of money."

# WORKING IN COMPANION ENERGY

**Winged Wolf:** "We are going to talk about working in companion energy. There is a flow to it, and there is nothing better for married couples than to work together on a project in companion energy. The best kind of project is actual physical labor, whether it be chopping and stacking wood together, or some other physical activity.

"Today, I would like you two (a married couple) to collect pine branches for Spirit's (Winged Wolf's horse) stall. Work together. I will not tell you how to work together, but find that point of flow that gives both of you joy. When you feel joy together, without frustration, then you will know that you are harmonizing, that you are in resonance with each other. Harmonizing is contrast, so, resonance is a better word. You are complimenting each other through your movements."

*Wings of Change: "Would you say again, the difference between harmonizing and resonance?"*

"Well, harmonizing is a complimentary sound of another pitch. I would rather have you resonating. This is a reverberation of the same sound, a flowing together, do you see? It is not one person being more dominant than the other. You are both equally dominant, relaxed, and happy. It cannot come if one person is pulling or pushing, and it cannot come if you are correcting each other for pulling or pushing. It can only come through the adjustment of flowing together. I want you to flow together in one big sweet movement.

"Even though one person might be using the chain saw and the other dragging branches, there is a flow to it and it works together. You will feel as one. Whoever is dragging the branches to the destination is but an extension of the person who is cutting them, and both will feel it. Do you see? It goes both ways. It is one sweet movement. It is an operation, two people in joy and balance together. Balance is very important. It will be a good practice session for you two.

"As you start out, the best way to get into that joyful flow of movement together is to be silent. Whatever you do, do not criticize each other or correct each other's movements. *Be silent.* Decide who is going to do what and do not let it matter, because it is all the same thing. Whoever is doing one thing this moment, may be doing the other thing the next moment. It turns, changes, and flows one thing into the other. Maybe one person is guiding the other person with the saw. It is all movement together.

"The two of you have no problem with your love. The love exists but you have not developed the joy of working together in an easy, easy flow. There are always little ripples, frictions, bites, and pricks because of your very different personalities. You are reaching a stage now in your spiritual development where the personality is becoming more refined, and its refinement is actually dominated by Soul, so, the little self is not important anymore. Who did what should not matter, do you see?

"This will be a practice session. There is no one who gets more glory than the other. Competition only gets in your way. Work from the Third Eye in silence, and move and flow together. As you do that, in that joy, you will notice your love takes on a grander scale. The grander scale is even lifted out of personal love, although that always exists. You will feel that you divinely or unconditionally love your spouse and, when this occurs, you will know that you are arriving. Your relationship is going to be transmuted into what you want it to be.

"This is my gift to you today. Explore its possibilities. Take it as far as you can.

"Be sure to start out in silence so that you begin to recognize the difference between superfluous words, which lead to misunderstandings, caused by the difference in your personalities. Establish balance, then the words you say have meaning to each other and upliftment. The difficulty the two of you have with each other, is that your words are chosen from personality. One has a more flippant type personality and the other is more subdued. When one person speaks with a flippant type of message, it is misinterpreted.

"So, you have to move beyond that. I want you to see the differences in your personality, not through exploration of words and bantering back and forth saying, 'Yes, but you said this and this means this.' You may do that on a psychiatrist's couch but here that will end up in a fight. What I want you to do is to explore it through silence and through getting to know the movements of the other person, through making your body flow with these movements as you produce this dance of joy, working in the field. It is a glorious experience working together."

# THE HAT AND THE FANTASY

**Winged Wolf:**  "Two in our illustrious apprentice family went down to the village and bought Aussie jackets and Aussie hats. When they came strutting out of the store, they looked like they were coming out of the outback of Australia. And you know, they had attitudes to go with it. They drove up to the gas station to get some kerosene and, lo and behold, the people inside the gas station leered at them from the windows saying to themselves, 'Uh, Oh, looks like we've got some Aussies from the outback, foreigners.' Either that or 'it's that California jet-set, you know how they are, always pretending. Well we've got to be careful of them. They have high and mighty attitudes. They think they are better than everybody else'.

"So you get kind of pegged a little bit. The lady from the gas station comes up and says, 'Are you going to tell me what you want or not?' Do you see? She gets a little irritated right off just to protect herself in case you are the jet-setter type that is out to make trouble on the island, or if you are an Aussie, well, she doesn't know anything about them, so she has to be a little leery there too. Either way, she has set herself up to protect herself and, of course, you guys were so much into the hat and the fantasy that you didn't really pay attention, except you wondered why the lady was not being nice to you.

"So much for fantasies. When you wear a fantasy, that fantasy is projected into the environment and other people look at that fantasy and, if they are not aware of what you are up to, they cannot laugh with you. They take it seriously.

"You were both aware of what you were doing, and you were playing, and I think that is wonderful. I am not suggesting that you should stop playing. I love seeing you strut around the property as Aussies. I think it's fun. When you go into public, go ahead and continue your fun, but be aware that other people may not know you are playing a game and having fun. They may not understand who you are. Your identity is mixed to them. Be aware of that. Maybe knowing this will make you a little bit friendlier or a little bit more sensitive to their uncertainty and you will try to put them at ease. Do you see?

"Fantasy is a problem within our environment in a great big way, because out there in the world, everybody is caught up in the fantasy of their own minds, their own myths.

"The body is a reflection of the type of person that comes into the world. You can see by the looks of one's body and by listening to what comes out of them, to see what is projected through their body. You can see that they have developed a self that is separate from the body, which in many cases is kind of wonderful because, for example, a very timid looking body does not necessarily have a very timid personality. Some people may look like they are introverted and yet, when you start interacting with them, you see that they are powerful characters. Their faces appear determined and their projection is self reliant. It can be quite a surprise.

"The mass consciousness has definitely evolved. These people have developed past the mental state they were born with. If they were to translate or die today, they would probably come back with a somewhat different body, to reflect what they had become. When you see people at a distance, and then you see them up close, it is very different. For instance, you, Standing Turtle, you are a very powerful lady, but what people first see is not always power. In your Aussie uniform they do see power. They think, 'Oh, this is the lady that kicks walls'. You see, that is what the Aussie uniform looks like on you. It is like, 'Say

93

something wrong to me and I will give you a little stomp on the toe', or something like that. (laughs).

"Life is complicated now. People are changing and you can see it. Their mental attitudes are actually displayed through their body language and on the expression on their face. People are not necessarily as they look anymore.

"Twenty or thirty years ago life was simpler. People matched the type of bodies they were wearing. It used to be that a woman who looked a certain way, was pretty, and one who did not look a certain way, was kind of plain. The same for men. Do you see? The plain now became exotic through the mental states they are carrying.

"So getting back to the fantasy and the hat, it depicts a mental state and people are out to try on different mental states to see what they feel like. This is one cause of the crime wave in our society. People are trying to adjust how they feel about themselves, and some people are looking for a way to present themselves differently.

"So people are trying on all kinds of roles and masks. People liked making masks of their own faces. The masks they make look like their faces, yet they do not look like their faces. Another quality comes through. They put on different qualities to see what it feels like. Street life has become like a Halloween Ball. On Halloween, people can seem a little scary. I went to the mainland last Halloween. All the clerks in the grocery store were dressed in costumes. Some of them had really hard core, rough looking exteriors. They were presenting images of machoism, cruelty, or crudeness in all different kinds of images. I found myself looking away, because the role they were playing, became real, as they got into it for the day.

"I saw one young man who was packing groceries with an army camouflage suit on. His face was painted for combat. He looked frightening.

"When somebody is wearing a costume and they are projecting an image, they are not only making a statement about themselves for that moment, but they make a statement about the role they are playing. The lady in the gas station had every right to feel that something was different. She might have seen you before but, 'Hey, who is this person really?' You know, it is fun and it is funny, but you should understand her point of view.

"You have to joke with her about it to bring her into your fantasy so she can be a part of your fun and she can enjoy it with you. If you are in a strange town and know you will never see her again, that is different, but now you might find that even if you go back again in your regular clothes next time she will still act a little strangely toward you.

"So this is part of what goes on in fantasy but it continues on at even a little deeper level. *People carry fantasies in their minds and they hide behind them.* Even though they do not wear a costume, they begin to dress up in the corner of their minds, and then they begin to act it out silently. Maybe they are Zorro in this little corner of their minds where nobody can see.

"Sometimes parents brag about how wonderful their children are, but the children cannot live up to the standards their parents have set for them. As a result, a child may begin to put himself down, building a myth of inferiority and incompetence.

"People who are called 'stupid' all their lives could rise above that stupidity by building an opposite images of themselves. On the other hand, they could become angry and defensive, which is why the path is difficult.

"There are also people who have not been beaten down but always feel like they are a little less than

95

everybody else, and they are angry about that. They get all caught up in anger for anger's sake. Anger then becomes a habit. They learned that if they look a certain way, they will frighten the person they are with, and they acquire power over others that way. I had an apprentice here recently who had that type of demeanor. She threw anger to get what she wanted.

"Her anger presented a myth or fantasy, and that fantasy is perpetuated, which made it difficult for her to live as Soul. It also made it difficult for her to live a real life, because she was totally controlled by the fantasy. It became a habit over a period of time. That is what fantasies do. You wear them for a period of time and you become them. It is the same as the Halloween costume you put on and you take off. Most people wear a costume because they have a bit of that quality, or they want to develop it in themselves, and that is fine. But when one's habits get carried away, mental habits like anger or poverty that get you an undesirable reaction, you begin to limit yourself and the fantasy becomes a real road block. It stops you from doing what you want.

"There is no point to life, if we cannot eat the cake that we have. Stifled, people begin to cheat themselves, which in turn, develops anger belts towards other people because they feel cheated. They are blaming others and doing it to themselves.

"Wearing an Aussie hat is a statement, and if somebody likes the statement, maybe they may relate to it themselves, they would think it is fun. While I do not relate to it, I know you two do, and I think it is fun. See, Turtle has got her Aussie hat on right now. Look at her.

"Your children see you one way, friends who have been important in your life have seen you another way, and you see yourself in still another way. When all this becomes integrated, then it will be pretty much the same. People will not necessarily understand you, because they

96

can only understand you according to their own state of consciousness, but they will have a *sense* of you, a sense that you are fair or you are unfair; that you are an okay person or you are not an okay person. They will have a sense of who you are and that is the important part. This is why I say, when you are out of character, when you are play acting, let the other guy in on it. Do you see? If you do not have any other association with that person, then it may not matter as much. You can blame it on the friend you're with by saying, 'I am with him'. You become the tourist. (Laughs).

"People here on the island are getting an image of Sky Wolf too. At first they just had an odd image, 'Oh, here is someone that is deaf. How different'. And then the more they are around him, the more they can see what he is like. For example, when he goes into the hardware store, he studies each item before he buys it. They can see how intelligent he is and how careful he is. They can see the involved mental state he carries. They can watch his body language and see what a strong interior he has. The mental state he carries is very strong. So, they begin to see that and then they say, 'Oh, I would like to learn sign language', because that is a way for them to get to know him better and communicate with him better. It is a real compliment.

"This is how communication begins. People interact and watch. They may not be consciously watching at first, but they observe as they interact.

"You are solid looking people. You are mentally balanced. You are kind. You are intelligent, and you are not caught up in fantasy. There is nothing frightening about you. Sky Wolf may not hear, but he is not a frightening person at all.

"Be aware of the fantasies you have so that, when you make a presentation into the world, you will know

97

what you are doing and the world will know what you are doing, so that the outcome will be as you want it to be."

*Two Eagles: "I have a new awareness of the importance of including others in one's fantasy, whatever it may be."*

"Otherwise they will resent you, won't they? It comes across that you want to brush them off as unimportant."

*Two Eagles: "Which is not true."*

"Which is not true, *ever*. There is nobody more important than another person. Each person in life is number one. Nobody is ever second to anybody else, nor should they be! This is very important. This is what Divine Love is all about. It is never looking at yourself as better, because you are not better. You may be more aware, but that does not make you better. It just makes life easier for you."

*Two Eagles: "It also makes me more compassionate for those who are not as aware, because I see their struggle."*

"Through being a part of life you pass on a little bit of your joy. That is a nice way to be."

*Two Eagles: "I have a question unrelated to the talk this morning. If one is deaf or blind, does that state alter their perception of time?"*

"Time is an illusion so it can only be perceived. Yes, it does alter it very definitely. To Sky Wolf, silence has movement to it. He has learned to mark time through that silence. Someone who hears, may mark time through sound and sight.

*Two Eagles: "Would that mean that he could regain his hearing?"*

"It means that one could no longer be deaf. Regain hearing? He has not had hearing in this lifetime. It means he would acquire the ability to perceive sound. He would relate to the sound of the Void and once the perception of the sound of the Void came, who knows? If a blind person could perceive, not intellectually, but actually perceive that all darkness was really light, so intense that it became darkness, he could no longer be blind.

"It is a state of consciousness that sees darkness as detached from everything, as separate and aside. That is what keeps a person blind. Once darkness becomes integrated with the rest of life, it is no longer darkness. This is where a miracle comes in to play. A miracle is truly a changed consciousness. When that consciousness is able to perceive that which it is not, it becomes changed. It becomes the state of illumination where it becomes that which it was not..

"So, that is how the blind see and that is how the deaf can hear. Unfortunately, there are people who have gifts of both sight and sound, yet they can neither see nor hear, because they are so wrapped up in their internal dialogue, their own fantasies. They have made a mess of their lives. I am not saying that they are stuck with that mess. They can get out. First, to get out of a mess, what do you have to do? It is the same as the blind person seeing, and deaf person hearing. You have to become aware of the fact you are in a mess, and that the mess is really order in chaos. This is very important."

Two Eagles: "So whatever is present, is the order of the moment, the recognition that this is the order, is then the key to moving on."

"Yes. When blind people become aware that the darkness of their life is really brightness and light, and not darkness,

99

except that it is so bright it becomes dark, they are no longer blind.

"When timid people look at their timidity and no longer see it as lack of confidence, they are no longer timid. When people who have been living in poverty no longer see their lack of money as being poor, they are no longer in poverty.

"An old friend once said to me, 'I grew up in a family with nine kids. We never had money but we never looked at ourselves as poor'. Therefore, none of those children ever grew up thinking about lack and they all have quite a bit of money today. So, the myth of not having, was not perpetuated, because it never was a myth to them to begin with. You see, the state that they had no money could not be perpetuated as a myth.

"Silence is really all sound, whereas all sound is silence in stillness form; but in the stillness you can mark time. Everything is there. All the ingredients of sound are there, but to someone who in a lifetime has never heard, to describe sound is very difficult, and yet it is there in the silence."

*Standing Turtle: "A shift in consciousness?"*

"Yes, a shift in consciousness. Now we are transmuting energy through perception and that is what Soul does. It directly perceives."

*Two Eagles: "It bypasses all the myths."*

"The Consciousness sees the myth. It might use the myth, It might put on the Aussie hat. Do you see? It might go strut around and play with it. 'Hey, I am pretending I'm an Aussie today', but It is aware of all the energy that It contacts while It is playing a part, and It makes sure It does not create little difficulties while It is doing it. Why would It want to?"

"Be aware of the fantasies you have so that when you make a presentation into the world, you will know what you are doing and the world knows what you are doing."

# MAKING YOURSELF HEARD

**Winged Wolf:** "Sometimes you make yourself heard by becoming invisible. Remember when you were in school and you would hide behind the person's head in front of you? 'Well, she won't see me'. So, you make yourself heard through trying not to be seen. That is pretty tricky, but either way, it is manipulation.

"When you reach the stage in your spirituality that you become so integrated with the flow of life; that you are both there and not there, you become a vital part of the flow. This means that your absence makes a hole, not because you stuck out among others, or were so visible, or that you were trying to impress other people. It means that you are a functioning part of the flow and ONE with that flow. In that way you are also ONE with whatever is going on. You are ONE with the teacher. When you become so completely ONE with something, then it just is. Then there is no box to contain it. There is no hard shape that says this, that, or the other thing is a certain way. Limitations are put aside. You simply become the flow Itself.

"So, there is no hiding involved. There is no pretending involved, because you cannot really pretend anything. There is only a total giving of yourself to the flow. The flow is the movement of life that exists in the space you are in. It is whatever exists in that space you are in. If you are at work, you become one with that flow. If you are the leader at work, you become the energy of that flow. You are so much IT, yourself, that other people begin to flow with you, with your wholeheartedness. You see, it is your love and your devotion to what you are doing that attracts. Devotion is not a concept or an idea, but a ONENESS, which is totally giving yourself to each moment. Permitting the aliveness of each moment to be

ONE with every movement, every action, every thought. It is total givingness and a total receivingness. When you give so totally, you can receive so totally.

"When you can give so totally of yourself, all that you have given, and all of the intent of your giving, the impact of your quiet mind, returns to you in abundance. The abundance, or that which you put out, is *magnified* as it flows back, not because you wished it, but because it responds to natural law.

You represent my abundance through your spiritual evolvement. Every time you take a step, I move forward as well and, at the same time, when I move forward, you move forward. Do you see? There is not a set order to it happening this way or that way, it is a giving and flowing. Now that we are gaining momentum, this moving forward, this flowing, this motion within our spiritual family moves everyone ahead. This forward movement occurs in your place of business as well. Once that momentum is gained, you must never interrupt it. Don't say, 'But wait a minute, let's stop here awhile'.

"And if others you are flowing with hesitate, don't look back at them. That is their stopping place. Let them go. If you look back at them, you have slowed down. Keep going. Never look back at them. You hold back the whole, and you hold back the flow. *Never look back at those who stop.* If they return to us at another time, fine, you will feel their return in the flow. It will be wonderful if they catch up again, but that's up to them. Let them make their own decision.

"It is not an easy thing to do, because you can feel the tug when they stop. All the same, never look back. Never give them your attention. This doesn't mean that the history book (memory) does not contain images of them. It may. It may contain pictures or things they said. Certainly there will be memory recordings that people will speak of once in awhile but, when they do, just look at them and go on. It is not wise to stop and reflect. **Never look back.**

"When you look back at moments in your life, moments where you have gotten stuck in your life in some powerful past incident, while you are doing that, you were actually there. It keeps you stuck there for a moment, and afterwards there is always a little downpull, a little depression, a little wondering, 'Well, is this so great where I am?' *Never look back.*

"Never compare yourself with another person or thing. In business you might take a look at what other businesses are doing, out of curiosity for what their flow looks like, what the energy looks like, and see what ideas propelled that energy, but never view them as competition, to beat, or compare your business with. Do not compare. There is no comparison. The moment you try to compare yourself with another person, you have stopped the flow via interruption to intellectualize the difference between 'this' and 'this'. **It doesn't matter!**

"Allow your aliveness to bring aliveness to that which you are doing. It doesn't matter what someone else is doing. Accept yourself. Watch the energy flow in your movement. Is it energetic? If the energy is low then examine why the energy is low in your movement. Examine why the wholeheartedness does not exist.

You say, 'Well I am wholehearted'. If you *truly* are, then you have no concern of the results, they are automatic success. Isn't that wonderful? If you are truly one with what is going on, you cannot help but have what you want. So, don't compare, don't compete. Swim with the flow. *Never look back!*

"Many times people pass out of your life. These are people who have been friends for a long, long time. If they are people who are moving forward themselves, don't look back to where they used to stand. Don't look back to where you used to stand. Do you see? *Simply be **Now**.* Let that 'now' be enough. Leave the past alone. It is just dust. If you stick your finger in it, you will see that which you touch is just dust. It is dead. The friendship that you have with those people now is the evolution of what was. They may have grown in this direction and you may have grown in a another direction. There may no longer be a common denominator and, if there isn't, that is okay. You made your choice, they made their choice. Why should you regret their choice for them, or for you? Your choice is your choice. Their choice is their choice. Let them go. If later on, one of you picks up the thread of the other or there is a common denominator again, then you work from there. It's odd how life brings you together so that you will meet again. Work from there, but leave the past alone. All those fun times from the past are in the past. They do not have anything to do with Now.

"One place where families get into trouble is in reminiscing. Arguments and ill feelings begin in reminiscing, that is, looking backwards, gazing into moments that transpired, that were seen through individual realities. Conflict arises. 'No, it wasn't that way, it was this way'. Or it arises out of unspoken conflict, 'They don't understand me'. *Leave it alone.* Don't drag it up.

"Touch only the present moment. Become so alive to the present moment that you move in flow with it. It will take you to the next moment, and your wholeheartedness will fulfill the next moment in the way that you want this moment to be. There is only This Moment! The past is dead. The future is a bubble. There is Only This Moment. Are there any questions or comments?"

*Wolfsong: "What is my consciousness if I'm peeking into the past or peeking into the future, and neither of them really exist.?"*

"A meddler. You are meddling in something that is dead, (past) versus something that could be, so they are both dead. By accepting that which had been and what could be, you then come into your present moment in a fantasy sort of way. This is where people get into the greatest difficulty, in manufacturing fantasy. They take the past, and they take what they want in the future, and they try to glue it together to this present moment which makes a mess out of the present moment. It makes a recipe of images that are not truly connected, yet they connect, because that is the way they want it to be - The past, to the present, to the future... They make this little recipe out of how they want it to come out, and it is called *manipulation!* So the moment of the present never has a chance to mature properly, to show its reality. It becomes a distortion of those past and future reflections that spill into becoming another moment of the present. But, you see, it never does, because it is always the present. The present takes form in the image of the past and the future. It never looks quite right. It is like a mutation. It's a pretty picture here with a lot of ugly little splotches on it, or distorted splotches. Do you see? The splotches are something you hadn't yet added on, and when you put the two together that is what happens.

"Now, if you live purely in the Void, you live this moment and this moment is allowed to become whatever it is that you carry inside of yourself. That is what life is. This life that you carry inside of yourself is growing in its aliveness as you are living this moment. Allow that to *become.* If that aliveness, as it is growing in you, is going to manifest into being a millionaire, then it will do that. Do you see? That does not mean that you don't take action along the way. Along the way always exists in the present moment, because the aliveness you carry inside of you is destined to reach for the Shaman Consciousness. There is nothing for you to do but to be wholehearted right this moment, to be so totally given to the moment that nothing else exists. Then, it is becoming. If the aliveness you carry inside of you is to have a family and children, that aliveness exists inside of you and, as you live that aliveness, it becomes. *So, there is nothing else but this moment. Allow the moment to fulfill itself. Get out of the way. Let it be!*

"There are so many little reflections to each thing that we talk about, so many different sides to it, so to speak. Only it is not a side, it is really a little reflection, a little image that comes back from each of you that you are carrying inside of you and that is what we speak to. That is what is existent in the moment and that is why what is to be said can never be premeditated, because as the speaking occurs your little reflections appear there and your little reflections appear here and so on. Each person's reflections appear and they get spoken to as they present themselves. A word presents a reflection that then goes to the speaker to address. The premeditation would be reaching into the future to say, 'Oh, so and so will want to know this'. Maybe when you are making the same talk day in and day out to an audience that is coming to you for a specific type of seminar, that kind of thing happens automatically. Do you see? We are not operating in that way. This is not a seminar. This is a moment of aliveness and it is taking shape as it is presented from me and from you."

*Two Eagles: "The notion of not competing and not comparing in the business world is a foreign concept. It should have a chapter in the book."*

"Yes, it would be a good chapter. Make it a separate one. We could talk about it now too, but you said it was a chapter, so the image then that came up, made it separate and that could be. But, it is also a moment right now that we could take to look at it. Maybe that separate chapter could come at another moment of aliveness.

"Competition in business: There is no point in trying to beat somebody out because life is eternal abundance. There is no lack. There is no limited supply of anything except in peoples' minds. That is where the limited supply is. Why do you need to push the other guy out?

"I learned from a dear friend in business about competition. He was a negotiator and he traveled around the world teaching people how to get along with each other in the business world. He often had people come to him who wanted to start out in the same business. I watched him. He never turned anybody away. He always took an appointment with anybody who came to him wanting to learn the business, and he did everything he could to help them get started. I questioned him one time, 'Well you know, he could be taking your clientele'. He said, 'Well if they do, they do. There's plenty of business to go around. I can't possibly do it all'. There was someone who understood the flow! Maybe not in a spiritual sense, but he understood it in his life.

"There is no end to it. That person lived an abundant life, never doing without financially. His personal business always flourished in many avenues, because he always had a keen eye for a new gimmick and a new idea. Because he wasn't afraid of helping people, he became a part of all these little projects. You see? He's probably a multimillionaire.

"So you don't need to compete. You need to just do your own thing. Now, if you want to be 'number one, up in the limelight', then I guess you are competing. But, to do anything for that purpose, is limiting yourself because you say it has to be in this image or not at all. So you are not going with the universal flow. And remember, the universal flow should not be a thing outside of yourself. You are to be the universal flow yourself, but to be that, you cannot be grabbing this way or that way because every time you grab in a direction, and every time you compete, you have actually stopped the moment. You have tried to hold onto that past instant so this little battle, this little war of competition can go on, and you have stopped the flow. You have put up a dam. So why compete? When you get out there running a marathon, don't care who gets ahead of you. If you are so worried about who is going to get ahead of you, you won't be able to enjoy your race. Maybe you will come out first. Maybe you will come out tenth. It doesn't matter unless you are counting who is the best. Well, the numbers don't say who is the best. The size of the smile at the end of the race says who is the best! *The joy that a person can live in life says who is the best. The freedom that each person experiences... that belongs to who is the best.*"

*Wings of Change: "So running a wholehearted race is the intention, rather than running the race either to win or beat your last time. Do I understand that?"*

"I would like to know exactly what level you are talking about. Intention is important in the material world but the path of a Spiritual Warrior is beyond intention. I have no intentions of anything.

"When you are living as a Spiritual Warrior, you do not concern yourself with intent. You let all the barriers go. You don't care. I mean you care but you don't care. Do you see? *You care in that you are one with it so there is a caringness but there is not a caringness to the point of concern about it.* There is not a fear of this or that. If you want to become something you must give yourself to it. You get in that flow and you do it. If you are so concerned in business about the competition, you are <u>not</u> giving yourself to what you are doing because your concern is for the competition and not for the moment you are living. That part of the moment that you are living has no aliveness to it. It is dead, fixed on an image of

109

something that you saw in a magazine or a newspaper, which said something about some other business, or it was something that somebody planted in you and said, 'Oh, have you heard about so and so?' If your emotions are hooked, you have a moment of deadness in this moment. You have given your power away to that competition.

"This is 'fine line stuff', but we are speaking from the viewpoint of someone who is living as Soul. I doubt that someone who is not prepared to live as Soul could possibly do it. If someone is not living as Soul, they are then living out of their mental baggage which would make it impossible not to get caught up in all that because that is what mental baggage is. Mental baggage is competition. It is manipulation. It is boxes and rigidness. It is all those little bits and pieces of things. There can never quite be any wholeheartedness, because you start wholeheartedly here and you get distracted. Do you see? You are always being pulled in two directions. Mental baggage always pulls you in two directions.

"It is the man or woman who totally give themselves to their work but at the same time feel guilty because they are neglecting something else. Maybe they are neglecting their children, or their husband, or their wife. There is always conflict in mental baggage. The person who lives from mental baggage cannot live as Soul. He cannot live wholeheartedly. There is always conflict and there is always pain to it. There is pleasure but there is not joy.

"Pleasure and joy are always different. Pleasure is a moment of laughter, kicking up your heels, a moment of sitting back and putting your feet up on the desk saying, 'Hey, this was a good day'. That is pleasure.

"Joy is when everything is okay no matter what happens, because you are one with what is happening. Isn't that spectacular? You can choose and you have chosen the life of the spectacular. That is what is becoming in your life, the spectacular. If you are enjoying the company of another person, that moment is so wholehearted, it is pure joy, pure companion energy. It is not one person competing with another. It is complete sensitivity. This is real love. This is a union with the moment and that is better than anybody's fantasy."

*"The abundance of that which you put out is magnified as it flows back, not because you wished it, but because it is natural law."*

# SUPPOSITION AS MANIPULATION

**Winged Wolf:** "May the blessings be.
"Did you sleep well last night, Sky Wolf?"

*Sky Wolf: "I had many different dreams. I would awaken suddenly, then go back to sleep and dream a different dream. There were flashes of pictures."*

"Did you hear anything?"

*Sky Wolf: "No."*

"Did what you see make you uncomfortable, the way you feel when you go out into the world?

*Sky Wolf: "Yes."*

"I often feel uncomfortable when I go out into the world, too. It is very noisy out there. You are lucky you do not have to hear it, but you see all this. Maybe it is better to know what is said. It is interesting that you had a dream like that, since all the quiet here makes you remember the noise. Well, when you have your holiday today, and there is much noise outside.." (laughs).

Ichinen arrived and went around to each person to be petted, stopping at Winged Wolf for a second generous helping. Winged Wolf commented,

"There are lots of ways of making love. This is one of them, and we three are participants."

*Standing Turtle casually says, "Is it supposed to be a certain way?"*

"There are no 'supposed' and 'suppose to's in life. Supposition is an opinion or an attitude brought on that forms an opinion. Supposition means that you are taking sides, this thing over that thing. You are having a preconceived idea of what an outcome is, do you see? So, you cannot suppose anything, or say it is supposed to be some certain way.

"You have to live without expectations. This is why I always say to you, when people come here to visit, they must come without expectations, because if they have an idea of the way they feel it *should* be, or the way it is *supposed* to be, that is fantasy. It will not be what you expect, nor can it be. There is no 'supposed' in residence here, this means that the word supposition, the act of 'supposing, or assuming, or expecting', does not exist here. It does not exist in Shaman Consciousness.

"You cannot suppose something and live in Shaman Consciousness. Now, you can use the phrase, 'I suppose so,' when you do not know the answer to something, but, be careful. You don't really 'suppose so'. Try to use more exact words. 'Suppose' itself is not an exact word, is it? It is a 'suppose', well, it could be, or it could not be. But the way you used it, was a declaration as if something were a fact, and there is no such thing.

"The only fact, the only reality, is that Soul is, God is, and Life is, Life being the dream of Soul, and Soul being the dream of God. Other than that, nothing exists. So, all the breakdowns of 'supposing this' and 'supposing that' come from a person's mind.

"So, there is no hardened fact to anything. The hardened fact is that Life is, Soul is, God is. We are God coming into Soul, into a human form. There is the power to present, but do not manipulate with that power. *Never* manipulate! That is the hardest part to get through to anybody, the non-manipulation.

"Supposing is a manipulation. Supposing something to be true is a manipulation, because you are supposing it. You are trying to make something a statement of fact that is not a fact, so you are trying to manipulate it into that little box. Do you see? There is no such thing!

"The word 'manipulation' takes a lot of forms. This is why I say visualization is manipulation. It is trying to conjure an image into a certain form. The Shaman Consciousness does not do that. The Shaman Consciousness chooses and fuses with that choice via direct perception. A choice is the object of one's attention, which, enlivened by Soul, manifests as the form of the decision. The seed is carried in your consciousness.

"That is why I speak very simply and very directly. Do not suppose anything. Do not live with expectations. Do not go anywhere expecting everything to be a certain way and then be disappointed. It is silly to be disappointed in life because disappointments do not exist. Expectations are an illusion, an illusion created by the mind for supposing that things should be a certain way.

"It is noisy out there. It is noisy because people are supposing this should be this way and that should be that way. They are trying to work through the day, getting other people to do things the way they think it should be done. You see a lot of chaos because there is manipulation going on. It is the manipulation that makes life so chaotic.

"You, being a spiritual warrior, or becoming a spiritual warrior, relax! Walk out there and stay in your energy capsule. Do not get involved in it."

# REFINING THE PERSONALITY

Wings of Change briefly mentioned being fearful of rejection. Accordingly, Winged Wolf directed her to sit 10 ft. away from the circle and said, 'I reject you. Please turn your back to me."

**Winged Wolf:** "May the Blessings be.
   "The fear of rejection, of losing your individuality, has controlled many of us for most of our lives. When the churches said that you are Soul individualized, you felt comforted, thinking that you still maintained that individuality which was so different than everybody else. The only individuality you have is your karma and how that karma stacks up. You know, it has such a great many combinations. You can take one instance of karma and make it interchangeable, maybe four hundred seventy-two million combinations to each piece. So, in this sense, you are individualized, but only as your karma dictates. As Soul, we are ONE. I am no different than you, you are no different than me. We are just ONE. We are all the same. There are no little pieces to the pie. I carry Soul to animate my body and I also carry the karmic circumstances that I have earned throughout lifetime after lifetime, just as you do. And there we have our individuality. Big Deal!

   "To say I reject you or I accept you, really does not mean much on that scale. How can you reject Soul? You and I are the same. So, the rejection is only on a personality level, isn't it? Again, big deal. Who cares? If the personality is rejected, maybe it needs a little refinement. If it is rejected by somebody else, it means it does not suit their personality. So what? You are still the same as that other person. You are still the same as me. We are all the same.

"I know that these are merely words, until you truly realize we are all the same. We are no different, except in body and karma. And your body is your karma too. Whether you earned a male body or a female body, whether it looks this way or that way, it is a composite of your karmic image."

*Easy Walker: "Is your personality also a composite of karmic influences?"*

"Absolutely, but most of your personality comes from your mother and father, and what you make of the two of them put together. Now, what you make of the two of them put together combines your mother and your father, with what comes in from past lives which is the third ingredient. And, what you make of your mother and your father put together, is what comes over from past times.

"Now, it could be that you had a strong relationship with your parents in past times, as well, which is usually the case.

"We have known each other in so many lives, it makes no sense to concern ourselves with acceptance or rejection."

*Easy Walker: "As an adult, what about the significant others in our life and their effect on our personality? Do they become a composite of our personality?"*

"Well, you try to identify with them, and in your efforts to identify with them, you take on little pieces of them. You say, 'O.K., this is me. I like this part. I am going to mimic this part. Or, I can't stand this part and yet, you mimic that too. Do you see? So karmically, you take on a lot of facsimile images. You grab at traits from other people, as well as things you have seen. For example, kids practice in a mirror how they are going to look. They pose so that they know how to tilt their head, move their hands and do different things in a manner in which they have seen that seemed neat. These then become facsimile images that they carry. Each one of us carries some of these images. They are looks and manners of doing things we have taken from people in the environment. These personality bonds fall away when you become aware that you are living as Soul. Suddenly, that part that you took from people and things drops away. It cracks like old dried up clay.

"Your natural personality, which evolved from your parents and yourself, from past lives, comes into fruition, and it becomes more refined. Then you begin to really see the influences as they come into your life. You really see who your mother is and how she is a part of you. You really see who your father is and how he interacts as a part of you. You see how you put the two together. And, when you develop this awareness, the personality starts to get refined. There is no judgment to pass anymore. There is acceptance and knowingness of how your personality came about. When this happens, you can then, 'put this down because it no longer serves you, or you keep it because it does.' You begin to develop wisdom. You can now begin to see who you really are. Until you see who you really are, there is no wisdom. There can't be wisdom if you are too wrapped up in what other people want you to be, or what you think they want you to be. That part has to be put aside."

*Easy Walker: "Does refinement of the personality become the natural personality itself?"*

Yes, natural. You become authentically natural. You are very comfortable. We are speaking about becoming comfortable, comfortable as Soul versus comfortable as a personality. We are not talking about comfort in how you are sitting or that you are comfortable in your habits. We

117

are speaking of comfortable as Soul, because you know who you are and you are not fettered by who you have been, or what people expect of you. This is what freedom is all about. There can be no rejection. There is no failure. There is no way to fail. *There is no way you can fail.* If you are living impeccably in the moment, the next moment has to be impeccable, because it is the fruit of the labor from this moment, do you see? This is how life becomes refined. It becomes so clean. The stress falls away that way.

"So yes, you are individual. You are an individual in your set of karma. As Soul, though, you are just like me and I am just like you. That is why it is very easy, when you are living as Soul, to look at someone and see what is going on with the personality. The rest is just like you. There is no guess work involved. It is just that the illusion is clearer. You perceive the energy. **What is, is**."

*Easy Walker: "Feelings of rejection are self imposed then?"*

"Self imposed or imposed by another personality who says, 'I don't like it, because you don't do this'. But, it is still self imposed if you accept it as that. Why accept it? Who cares? You can go into town and I am sure there are people who would like you and there are also people who would not like you. Do you see, who cares if they like or don't like you? If you are being natural, authentic in yourself, you are not doing anything to harm them. They are just scrutinizing you from their personality. So, you should have compassion for them since they don't realize that they are really scrutinizing themselves. You are their mirror. Why concern yourself? The good old 'little self'. But, the 'little self' stays a part of you, even though you pass beyond being controlled by it. It is always a part of you. You use it as a tool to function in the world. But it becomes so refined, it does not have many little querks to it."

*Easy Walker: "Because the personality becomes more evolved, why do we still use the term 'little self?"*

"I accept that corrected choice of words. The 'little self' does not become evolved after awhile."

*Easy Walker: "So, it is all about the refinement of the personality?"*

"Yes. As Soul, you are comfortable, really comfortable. Life is fun and exceedingly joyful. It is a love affair with life.

Speaking to Wings of Change, still seated in the back of the Happy House with her back turned,

"So, how does it feel to feel rejected down there?"

*Wings of Change: "I don't feel very rejected."*

"Oh! Well, isn't that wonderful. Good for you. Why don't you come back and join us.
        "Feeling rejected is really dumb, isn't it? I mean, you can't be rejected, because it doesn't exist. Rejection does not exist. It is just a memory from childhood, the school day things.
        "You were probably the most popular person in school, and worked very hard to be that."

*Wings of Change: "Maybe not quite the most popular, but I worked hard to be that."*

"And that's your biggest hole. When you get beyond that, you will get what you want. Isn't that a bust?"

*Wings of Change: "Yes."*

"Every Sage apprentice has one great big hole, but each person's hole is an illusion. Their hole at its darkest, is all light. Once you get beyond the illusion, you naturally turn your attention away from it. And, the way you get beyond it is by not caring about it, by just being totally bored by it. 'Oh no, not you again. That dumb old fear of rejection again. Oh, how boring'. Don't get hooked. You have to intercept it. Do that a couple of times, and it will let go.

"This means, if everybody in your study group says, 'Well, we like the study group except for you', it would be like, 'Oh No, I don't want to listen to this boring thing.' You don't have to please the world. You please me by being comfortable in yourself.

"You know, everybody has flaws in their personality. You will never find a personality that is just a bright shiny penny with no little black mark on it. I mean, 'Who Cares? So What? What is the big deal?' If they see your flaw it is because there is something they are seeing that is reflected back to them.

"When you go to places, you often hear people talking about other people. You don't hear them speaking about interesting things; and, you know, the weather is interesting. Listening to the sound of raindrops is interesting. They have unusual patterns. There are so many interesting things and textures in life. To discuss someone's personality? What a boring thing to do."

*Wings of Change: "Why do people spend so much time just picking.."*

"Because they are staring at themselves. They are staring at themselves, feeling that everybody is staring at them."

*Wings of Change: "I had a flash of an incident while in my cabin yesterday. When I was in grade school, we were in an auditorium and we were singing the national anthem. I remember we were singing and I loved to sing. Well, I noticed two schoolmates of mine were talking. When I looked back to them, they said, 'We were just discussing how involved you get when you sing.' The comment seemed like a little nasty thing..."*

"It doesn't sound nasty to me, but kids may think of it as nasty and maybe they meant it to be nasty."

*Wings of Change: "It was one of those memories that came up, over my fear, an attitude about wholeheartedness."*

"Oh, it was, 'I won't be that wholehearted again because what will they be saying, yet here you are on a path that demands wholeheartedness. Tough, isn't' it?"

*Wings of Change: "Yes, it is one of those long buried memories of being so sensitive to something, so insignificant."*

"Children are very much their parents at those ages. They are like parrots up to the age of about 15 or 16, and at that point, they start to pull out of it, which is why they are often at times so difficult. Suddenly, they turn on their parents in an effort to discover themselves."

"Wholeheartedness. One only achieves through wholeheartedness. If everyone sang the national anthem as you did as a child, there would be great patriotism. Such is the power of wholeheartedness. I would have applauded you."

# INTEGRATION

**Winged Wolf:** "The integrated personality or the integrated person becomes One with whatever they are doing. In the first stage, you begin to do something so wholeheartedly, that while you are doing it, you become One with it. That is the key to success - You become so wholehearted in what you are doing, it just IS.

"The integrated person, when they think something, or when a word pops out of their mouth, is in total alignment with that particular moment. What comes out of their mouth is the image carried in them.

"Now, many times words will come out of an integrated person that have nothing to do with images. They have to do with speaking from Soul itself. They are not premeditated. The spiritual person, who is integrated, does not live a premeditated life. They live a spontaneous life, which unfolds in the moment, and they speak according to what occurs in that moment. When they speak, they are totally One with what is happening.

"So you see, integration is not separation, it is Oneness, it is wholeheartedness, first. This is how you begin. If you want to step onto the path of being an integrated Spiritual Warrior, then first, become wholehearted, completely One with what you are doing. If you reach out your hand, you do it deliberately. If you want to take a horse blanket off Spirit, you are One with taking it off. The flow is an even, smooth movement. Practice wholeheartedness through your actions. Totally focus on what you are doing.

"At first, this may seem very difficult, but after awhile, it becomes easier. As it becomes easier, something occurs. Mental images you carry inside of you become One with whatever it is that you are doing, until gradually, there is no separation to anything anymore. You become an integrated being, integrated Oneness with All life."

Standing Turtle

# ONENESS

**Winged Wolf:** "The recognition of the Oneness with all life comes to you when you see yourself as light, and you see the light of all things. At that moment, the light you are perceiving is the Void. It is **the** One Light. It is you as the light, and every object as the light, and every person as the light. The light reflects the Void.

"Objects are presentations made by sentient beings. All objects therefore, contain light, because they are infused with the consciousness that presented them. All beings of light are energy. A rock is an energetic being. A rock is a manifestation of nature and, sometimes, rocks are manifestations of sentient beings.

"All objects are light. This building that we are in is an object of light. Its lightness is infused by those who built it. Even in its most crude form, it is light; otherwise, there could be no structure. Without light, there is no structure and yet light itself, has no structure.

"When you begin to witness the light of all things, you will know you have moved beyond the intellectual realm. You no longer simply intellectualize, 'Yes, all things are One'. You will visually see all things as One, and you will recognize who you are, Oneness with it.

"This is a very important step. The first time you recognize the Oneness as light, you will be in a state of mental silence, although later it may occur while you are animated. The first time will most likely come about when your body is still, not when the mind is asleep, but when it is simply relaxed and quiet.

"And, at some point, when I feel you are ready, I am going to help you by providing an environment for your experience. You have to get past the shocking part of your senses first, and hopefully, you will take the step soon.

"Remember, total darkness is brilliant light turned inward. Total light is darkness. So, when you witness the light of all things, and yourself as a part of that light, then suddenly, you see it doesn't matter if it transposes into darkness, because they are one and the same. No fear can exist in this state, because fear is caused by uncertainty of the unknown, and there is nothing that is unknown, even though there is still exploration to be done in the darkness, or in the brilliant light, whichever you want to call it. It continues forever. Fear, however, cannot exist there, because you are One with it, as well.

"So, to have this experience of Oneness, first comes a willingness to put fear aside, and the wisdom to deal with it, when fear confronts you in a horrifying way. When you experience the quiet stillness, there might seem to be a moment of horror. The moment of horror is the fear of the unknown. So, you need the wisdom to confront it, so you don't go crazy. That is why we take things in steps. Your apprentice journeys leads you further and further toward that goal.

"Finally, the right moment will come. This is what is meant by 'passing through the eye of the needle'.

"May the blessings be."

# MESSAGES FROM SOUL

**Winged Wolf:** "Messages from Soul: Intuition is Soul's messager. The body is a sensor. Intuition wears many pieces of clothing in that it speaks to us as energy running through our bodies, our bodies being our brains, our arms and legs, our torso, even our toes. When someone says something to you that suddenly strikes a chord, which makes a chill run through your body, it is a message to you. That message will verify itself to you as meaning something in particular. A chill running through your body may mean an agreement to what is being said. 'Yes, that is what I needed to hear.' That is Soul saying, 'Pay attention!'

"Now, a similar type of body feeling can come when you encounter something that tells you to be careful through fear. If you were to suddenly walk into a graveyard and become frightened, you might have a chill run through your body. But there is a distinguishing factor between the two chills. One chill is a comforting, reassuring chill that makes you pay attention, and the other is a freezing chill that makes you feel like you want to run away. So, you have to pay careful attention to the differences as they occur within your body, when you feel intuitional energy.

"There are still other types of sensations your body will give you, such as when you are a little nervous, or have anxiety. Some of you might have butterflies in your stomach. The experience of feeling butterflies in your stomach, can also happen when you feel an attraction to another person. So, here again, you have to learn to distinguish one type of feeling from the other. You may be anxious when you have to make a speech, or have a presentation to give in your business in front of an audience. The anxiousness gives you butterflies in your stomach. It is often called stage fright. Or perhaps, when you are eager to see someone, you will have butterflies in your stomach, as well. And that eagerness has a different feel to it than anxiety. Do you see? So we have to learn to distinguish the difference.

"The anxiety butterflies are like fear. The eagerness butterflies are like a wanting to go toward something, an anticipation. Now, they are both anticipation, but they have a different base inside. You will learn to distinguish the difference between stage fright and eagerness as you become more alert to your intuition or Soul nudges.

"There are other feelings that the body gets. If suddenly a headache strikes when you are in the presence of someone, you will know that you are being intruded upon by that person. If you are quiet for a moment, you can usually sense images of that person coming to mind. Remember, the brain is a part of the body. When the brain receives images, it is the imagination producing images as portrayed on the screen of imagination, by which it gives you messages. These are Soul nudges.

"Now, the headache itself is not a Soul nudge, it is an intrusion from another person. That could occur, for instance, at a business meeting. Somebody is there silently attacking you, and that silent attack suddenly strikes a headache. Having a headache like that, is like somebody sitting in the corner of your mind, your brain, scrutinizing, banging away, or attacking you. The person in your brain that is giving you a headache, is attacking some reaction that they have to you. It is a very strong reaction. So, pay attention to these headaches. If you find somebody gives you a headache, you might become watchful. Is it everytime you are in their presence, or is it just once in a while? Is it only in certain situations, or does it happen all the time? If you have a constant feeling of discomfort in somebody's presence, Soul has given you the nudge to leave. So leave! You have to learn to listen to signals in your body.

"There are other types of signals. If you are living with someone and you are constantly sick, or if everytime you are around someone in particular, your body gives you some kind of sickness signals, the same thing is happening. You have been attacked, and you have a choice at that point. If you remain in the situation, then you are remaining by choice. If you unconsciously allow this to happen, you are allowing yourself to be a victim. Be careful about playing the victim role. Even though you are not really being a victim, if it's your choice, you are still allowing yourself to act out a victim's role. Do it very purposefully, if you do it at all. I do not advise anyone, unless they have a real agreement to take on somebody else's karma, to do it. Do not get sick for anyone else, because you can hurt yourself in many ways.

"Paying attention to all the body signals that are coming to you in situations that you experience in life, now, only occur if you, *as Soul*, are in tune with yourself. If you are living from a *mental* point of view, where all your emotions are intact, you are incapable of picking up on the nudges from Soul; that is, tracking feelings you are having in your body. By tracking your body feelings, you can stay healthy. By tracking nudges that come from Soul, you can protect yourself. You can perceive the energy that is coming at you. You can perceive the energy that exists in the environment. When you walk into a room, you know what is there and you make a conscious choice whether or not to be there, which removes you from the role of a victim. Unless you are living as Soul, you cannot do that.

"So, you have to learn what living as Soul is all about. We have said many, many times that it is living from the Third Eye viewpoint. The Third Eye viewpoint means letting go of your personal myth or letting go of the control your 'little self' projects, your personality's control

128

over your life, and giving that control over to Soul. You, as Soul, are aware of everything that is going on. But you, as mind, are very limited. One's mind is limited by experience and by emotional buttons that are implanted from memories in the past. And that is all emotion is, regurgitations from the past. So, what somebody says to you, can push a button to make you angry. If you were to really look at that anger, you would see that, a long time ago, you developed an attitude about a certain thing, and that attitude produced anger. So, you can see the difference here, between Soul nudges and that which comes from your emotions.

"If somebody says something to you that makes you sad or makes you cry, then you get really depressed. Depression, too, is another form of anger, and this emotion also comes from past experience buttons. If you will remember back into your childhood, or somewhere in the recent or distant past, you will discover an attitude or an opinion that built up a 'body feeling' about the opinion or attitude, and that 'body feeling' said, 'depression'. Do you see? So every time someone would say something to you about that, you would strike this depression chord, or maybe you would get defensive or, from your idea of love, a love button might be pushed.

"Real love is not an emotion. People today speak of love as an emotion, because they tie love feelings into their body. What they are really talking about is the pleasure, and pleasure is an emotion. It is not a nudge from Soul.

"A button pushed in one's mind may be pleasurable, but pleasure does not reflect real joy. Pleasure reflects slapstick happiness. It is tied to whether somebody does something the way you want it. If that is pleasure and happiness to you, it is very *transient*. That type of happiness is here today and gone tomorrow. The type of joy we want in our lives is that which comes from Soul

129

perspective, a joy that is yours no matter what happens. You carry that joy inside of you. You **are** that joy. So, even though a lot of problems may come up, the joy part still exists, even though there are difficulties.

"You become self-sustaining. You are self-reliant. As Soul, you are ONE with yourself, and that much you always have. If all your possessions were to go, that would still not destroy the joy part of yourself. In a way, it would be okay, because you would know that you made the choice yourself, that you are not a victim. If you get carried away with someone else's idea of the way you should live, and *then* you lose everything, it is not joyful, is it? The decision was *not* from Soul. Here is the difference - you cannot maintain joy in a state where you allow someone else to live your life for you. This is very important. Most people do this because they feel that it is their responsibility to live to please others. This is not true. First and foremost, you must live impeccably and honestly, to please yourself in a kind and caring way. At first, it may not seem kind and caring, but soon others around you will begin to feel more comfortable, more fulfilled in your presence. This is because you are not weighing and judging situations, or living in conflict.

"First, however, you must become totally acquainted with your personality or your myth, and be willing to give up the fantasies in your life. Only then will you come to know who you are. Coming to know who you are is not easy. It is important that you have a teacher with whom you can work comfortably, as Soul. With your teacher at your side, you discover aspects of yourself for yourself.

"The process of recognizing yourself is probably the most difficult part of the entire spiritual journey, and sometimes very painful, because you have built up certain defenses about who you **think** you are. To give up those defenses, means you suddenly feel vulnerable, the object of other people's opinions, which, of course, is not true.

Family opinions may imply that if you change jobs, you are unstable. If you carry the idea that you are unstable if you change jobs, then changing jobs becomes very difficult, yet you say to yourself, 'Well, I don't want this job anymore. I want another job'. You have to go ahead and find that other job to please yourself, whether or not it is sensible in somebody else's eyes. It is your life that you are living.

"This does not mean that you just run here and there and live by whims. This is why this process is very difficult to do by yourself, without a teacher, because in the beginning you say, 'Well, I don't really like my job.' So, what do you do? You jump to the other end of the stick and want to jump from job to job to job. That certainly is not the answer. That is living from emotion, or living from your passions, rather than paying attention to what it is you really want to do.

"When you feel a strong passion to jump to the other end of the stick, you are better off staying exactly where you are, until that emotion settles down. Now, this is not to say that living as Soul is without passion. It is a most passionate life, because it is wholehearted. But here again, there is a difference from what is real passion, from passion that is led by one's emotions.

"People usually want to jump from one job to another to another, not because they are drawn to that new experience by a Soul nudge; but rather, because they are afraid to stay where they are, fearing something unfortunate may develop down the line. They are projecting into the future, getting confused and unsettled. Do you see?

"When people want to rush from one marriage to another, or rush from relationship to relationship, it is usually fear based. This may mean they become afraid when they reach a certain point in their relationships. The feeling is, 'Oh, I'd better start over again somewhere else.'

131

And so, they become attentive to body attractions from someone else, and then run in that direction. They think, 'Oh, this means I should go over here.'

"Living from a mental point of view or from an emotional point of view, is a trap. You spend your life running from situation to situation without really evolving. When Soul gives you nudges, when you are living from your intuitional body, when your body can respond in an intuitional way, because you are open enough to live as Soul, it is very, very different. You have many experiences in life, but when you step into the experience, one automatically leads to the next, without ruffles. Life is mostly joyful. There is not chaos and confusion.

"Remember, chaos only comes when you are living from your emotional body, when you are grabbing at things, when you are trying to make things happen. *That is manipulation!* Living as Soul, there is no manipulation. You live one hundred percent wholeheartedly in the moment, and the moment evolves. That way, you have no flack. You do not create negative karma and life is easier. It is better all the way around.

"You have to start by getting tuned-in to your body. Pay close attention to your body signals. Do not just grab at something. If you want to start without a teacher, what would you do? You could begin with a notebook. Every time you have a feeling in your body, write that feeling down. Of course, this means you are not going to have time to get out there and live life, because you are going to be sitting there writing down all these feelings. The difference between working alone and working with a teacher is that you can meet with that teacher periodically, and find out what it is that you have experienced. You will begin to notice things and the teacher can point out certain aspects of your myth that are tied to that experience. A teacher can sort it out for you, or help you sort it out. Or, a teacher can grab a handle on some part of your emotional body that is sticking out that you cannot see. When this occurs, you become more free to be tuned-in to your body."

Standing Turtle: "The brain is the body?"

"The brain is the body. I know most people look at the brain as not being a part of the body. It is the body. And, in one of your journeys, you make an extensive study of the brain.

"It is quite interesting how the brain operates, and **the** brain is the main message center for Soul, because all the feelings that go through the body are really feelings that are connected to different centers in the brain."

Standing Turtle: "How about the mind?"

"It depends on how you are using the word 'mind'. I seldom use the word mind because people have so many different ideas of what the mind is. In reality, when looked at in its purest sense, the mind would be an attribute of Soul. However, in the way that it is usually used, it is not that at all. It is put into a 'brain' type of category. Let's make three categories for the sake of understanding: the brain, the mind and Soul.

"The brain is a message center of accumulated facts, like a computer. It has data. The mind is what cognates what the computer knows. It takes the information from the computer, and interacts with that information and makes fantasies. So, the mind is a fantasy machine, the imagination. The brain is a machine of comprised data. The mind takes that data and with the use of imagination, puts together what the brain knows, combines it with fantasy, and it comes out with a picture of something. That picture may or may not be reality. Do you see? People say that reality is relative. It is true.

133

People's reality is relative on a mental level, but there is a true reality, which most people do not know about. You can only know about true reality from Soul viewpoint.

"So, this is a separate category, a separate subject that we need to talk about. Briefly, we have the brain, which is the computer, and then we have the mind, which takes the information in the computer, crosses it with different sections of the brain, and comes out with a fantasy through the imagination. And then we have Soul. Soul perceives the energy and knows what is reality and what is not.

"Now, mind in its purest sense; that is, the highest aspect, is relative to Soul; but, it is better that we use categories here so that you can understand. In Buddhism, they call it the chitta mind. The chitta mind is the highest mind, which would be the mind of Soul, but that gets very confusing for people when they start looking at it like that.

"The three categories, the brain, mind, and Soul, give you a general picture. The mind, as a fantasy machine, is the place where imagination reigns, where the seat of power of imagination is. This is where fantasy comes in, and this is where people get themselves in the greatest amount of difficulty. All these messages, or data, which is stored in the brain, can be embellished or fantasized in a million different ways through the imagination. This puts people in conflict, because of the fantasies they have created for themselves, from the information stored in their brains. This is *big time* and this is where the teacher comes in - to help sort that out. Those fantasies are called a person's myth, and the personality that they have developed out of that myth. Today, we have many strange people running around. Not that there were not always strange ones, but they are a little stranger now, and more plentiful, because of the fantasies that have developed through the evolution of the mass consciousness itself. Soul perceives all this."

# THE FALL OF SUPERMAN

**Winged Wolf:** "May the blessings be.

"What I'd like to talk about this morning is the Superman episode that we saw on television last night. There was a particular point in the story that directed us to pay attention to what happens when one gets caught up in emotions, our emotional bodies. Superman and Lois, or Clark Kent and Lois were to be married but she went off with another man. She went with another man Lex Luthor, because she had amnesia and thought the name Clark was the enemy, do you see? She said to Clark, 'I don't love you anymore, and suddenly Clark, who is actually Superman, is devastated and he allows her to leave with the character portraying the evil lord of the Universe.

"Superman's emotional body kicked in and his feelings got hurt. He lost all his power in that moment. He could not think of her safety. He could not remember that the man that she was leaving with was the evil lord of the Universe. You see, he couldn't remember any of that. He couldn't remember his bond with Lois. All he knew was that, when he found Lois without knowing what had happened to her, he accepted the words she said and it triggered his emotional body. As a result, he lost his power. His emotional body said to him 'she doesn't love me anymore', and he had flashbacks of perhaps rejection, or fear of rejection, because of who he was, do you see? He was this all powerful being, so how could he ever expect having a normal relationship anyway?

"So all his little fear things were triggered and he got caught up in his emotional body. His buttons were pushed and he stood there helpless, watching her drive away.

"You can see how a person's emotional body can control them. If it can control Superman, it can control you. You have to become conscious of your emotional butons. You have to be observe life as Soul, even though you become very much involved in life. Remember always that you are the *presenter* of life. If you get caught up, if you have somebody who has so much power over you, if you have given so much of yourself that if they look cross-eyed at you, you are so totally devastated, and your world crumbles apart, then you are being controlled by your emotions, and not divine Love.

"It is very important to never allow yourself to be controlled emotionally, and the only way you can be controlled, is emotionally. It is not love to be controlled in that way. It is fear of not being loved. Love itself knows no fear. And we're speaking now of divine Love. There is no fear in divine Love. It is an eternal foun-tain and you can never give it too much. There is no fear of it not being received, or how it will be received, because it is love. It's that clean. It doesn't have expectations or strings attached. It doesn't say, 'Lois this is Clark, your love. Come with me', do you see? It is not devastated.

"You cannot be devastated when you are on the Path of Soul, but you can be devastated with one foot dangling off. With one foot dangling off, you are susceptible to having your buttons pushed. Those emotional buttons are a part of humankind and they are always sitting naked. As long as you are on the Path of Soul, you cannot be touched by it. The minute you step off the Path of Soul, you're a goner. Once one button gets pushed, there's another button, and then that button connects to another button. There are so many buttons, they can just go on forever. Now, that is not to say you cannot see what you are doing and get back on the Path.

"This lifetime, any lifetime, the whole purpose of life, and there is no other, is to discover yourself as Soul, and to live omnipresently as a part of the Godhead. There is no other purpose. Everything that you do along the way is for the experience.

"Everything that you do along the way is to train you in the impeccable life. Everything that you do along the way is to train you to be wholehearted. Everything that you do along the way is to focus you on your path. Your path is the Path of Soul. It is the Path of Awakening, the Path of your Empowerment, FREEDOM! Real freedom, bound to no one. In this state, when you are bound to no one, you are completely free to love everyone and to give that abundant flow of love flowing through you.

"This is the state when life becomes easy. The effort to life goes out. You don't need it. You don't need effort. You don't need to struggle. You don't need to suffer. Now, that is not to say that we don't fall once in a while, but we fall less and less and less and less, because the more accustomed you get to living as Soul, the less accustomed you become to living without it. You become so accustomed to living as Soul, you look at life as Soul and you see the energy that is there. You see the illusion that is created by that energy and your choices are very clear. It's almost like it is an automatic choice just as it was an automatic choice when you were living in the illusionary world. You see, 'Oh, I have to have this, or I have to have that', is the illusionary world.

"But from the side of Soul, you look into the illusionary world and you participate in it as it is necessary, and as you so choose, becomes as it is necessary. They are the same. You choose to be of service to life, and that is as it is necessary and it is as you choose.

"It is necessary for you, as one who is living as Soul, to give to life, to live in service. It is impossible for you not to do so. If you would try not to do so, you would immediately be back into the illusionary world again.

137

There is no choice that way, but there is all choice. It is necessary for you to interact with the illusionary world in the tone of service, not fabricated service, but divine love service, where it is natural. It is a natural giving. There is no make believe to it. There is no fantasy involved, although you can participate in a fantasy to be of service. It is a choice and it is a necessity.

"So where does this all end? It doesn't end. It goes on and on and on. Your capacity to love divinely grows as you walk the Path. Each day you become more capable of this very magical, very wonderful, magnificent love. It becomes so easy. It becomes a natural part of you. You become that love yourself. It is not a separate thing that you are giving. It just is.

"Now, when you become an embodiment of divine love, then you become that energy that pulsates purely from the Void itself, pulsating into the world. If you go to the grocery store, then you are pulsating, not through any fabrication, but naturally pulsating as divine love. There is no ego attached to it at all, because you are in a state that is so natural and so comfortable that you don't stare at it. If you stare at it, then you are immediately a part of the illusionary world again.

"So, all of this brings us back to the starting point of this talk, which is - first, you get a handle on the emotional body. You recognize what effect it has in your life. You watch it work. You watch for the trigger. You watch it and you catch it. You intercept it, and your choice says, 'No, I'm on the Path of Soul. I am walking as Soul into life'. That's what the Path of Soul is'.

"At that point you begin to take total responsibility for yourself. You are self reliant. You are love personified. You are free and those around you feel the freedom that you carry within yourself, and it is natural that they will want to possess you. But, you cannot be possessed. This does not make you angry. If it made you angry, it would push you back into the illusionary world again. Your emotional button would be pushed. You simply perceive that energy, and because of its nature you do not care to participate in it. Life is easy. We'll stop here for today."

*"It is very important to never allow yourself to be controlled emotionally, and the only way you can be controlled, is emotionally."*

# LETTING GO OF FEAR

**Winged Wolf:** "Let the blessings be.

"If you have a habit of doing something that is disturbing to you, such as getting startled to the point that it makes everybody else startled, and it is just a habit, you can intercept that habit. If you intercept it one time, then you will intercept it the second time. After three or four times, there won't be a habit.

"Now, I would say you are well over twenty-one, so you should be able to have a grip on yourself by now. I want you to make a list of all the things that get you startled. You'll have to go back in memory and make a list of them all. Will you do that?"

*Wings of Change: "Yes, I will."*

"You are always afraid something is going to happen. You are seeing something happen that is not happening."

*Wings of Change: "Do you mean I'm making something up about the future?"*

"In the moment, you are. As a child, you probably had little monsters crawling out from under your bed. You let out these exclamations, and you're still seeing monsters! (laughs) Now, you have monsters coming out everywhere. What are you seeing? You have to pin it down to what you are seeing. Are you seeing little light forms?"

*Wings of Change: "No, the startle response can come out of a shadow crossing my path."*

"All right, so you are seeing light forms. Shadows are light in reverse. We have spoken of this before."

140

*Wings of Change: "I'm afraid the old bogeyman will get me."*

"I certainly will. (Everyone laughs) You are actually seeing little light forms, but they have no control over you."

*Wings of Change: "Why do they frighten me, then?"*

"Because you think they do. This is going to be fun. I get to be a bogeyman."

*Easy Walker: "You are to many already, probably. You know how you dangle things in front of people."*

"What do you mean I dangle things in front of people? Do you mean their stories?"

*Easy Walker: "Yes, that's like being a bogeyman, you know. Look at this!* (Easy Walker holds out an imaginary dangle)."

*Wings of Change: "Another way of saying it for me is that when I'm here in this space it allows all those things to show up. In the space of pure stillness, everything is reflected and whatever is popping up at the time is what shows up."*

"Now that you are living more and more in a quiet mind, you have stillness, however, then you see something and it has more impact and you let out your startle response. I know when I looked at you the other day your astral body actually jumped outside of your body. You stepped in front of me."

*Wings of Change: "Was there any meaning to that?"*

"Your astral body stepped in front of me. It was probably clinging for protection.

Wings of Change: "So what's the origin of bogeymen under the bed?"

"What kind of bogeymen under the bed? What kind of dreams did you have as a kid? What kind of recurring dream?"

Wings of Change: "My recurring dream was that everyone in the house turned into a lion or tiger and tried to eat me up."

"You can get rid of anything or you can invite anything."

• • •

"One of the things I'm going to ask you to do in your HUing is to acknowledge your own light body. When you sit down in this position, there is a light around you (points to different areas of our bodies) from the edge of your skin and extends out to about eight inches. I want you to pay attention to it while you are HUing. If you have your attention at the Third Eye, you will be able to perceive it. So you perceive that image of your light body around you. When you do that you will strengthen your light body. This goes back to the principle, that wherever you place your attention, that is what is magnified.

"You are not out to build the size of your aura. Do not manipulate it in any way. Just simply put your attention on it. When you do that, you will find you are living more and more inside of your own capsule, which is where your strength is. So when we HU you are pushing your energy out to the edge of your capsule. I know, I have said this many times, but I've never said it quite this way. At that point no bogey person could frighten you. The bogey people can't come in if you push your energy at the edge."

Wings of Change: "Does that mean there really are bogey people?"

"Well, there are bogey people that come from your mind. They might be lodged in there for a long, long time. Your bogey people could be living inside of you for forty or fifty years. Then all of a sudden little things happen and it's as though a button is pushed or a door opens and those bogey people jump out. But, if you are not living in your mind or your mind is not in control, this does not happen. Right now you are still vulnerable to the buttons, but if you are living inside of this capsule, with awareness of your light body, thus strengthening it, there wouldn't be any of those little things."

*Easy Walker: "Those little things that are in my mind are like fears; so, if you keep this capsule you still have them contained in your mind."*

"Well, the capsule exists all the time anyway. The only difference is, it is between having a door open or a door shut. You close the door, so, therefore, the mind is not going to be projecting those images or if it does you will simply look at them. Do you see? They are not going to have any power to control you, which is pretty wonderful."

*Wings of Change: "So, for clarification, it isn't that as a child who is able to see astral entities, you see things that frighten you, then forget about them and then later..."*

"Well, mostly, when you say astral entities, it is energy coming from your own self that you are seeing, do you see? You are the creator. You present it. Your brain is a great image maker."

*Wings of Change: "How do you know an image from Soul vs. an image from the brain?"*

"An image from Soul is deliberate. It is conscious. You set a target and you put your attention on that and it is. It is not visualization."

*Easy Walker: "Can you visualize when you are at the Third Eye, or is that what Is?"*

"There are pictures that come through the mind while you are at the Third Eye, so in that sense they are always occurring. You never get hooked onto those pictures, so they are free flowing. Now, sometimes it is necessary to stop and look at something. This is what we call the art of looking. We'll freeze frame a picture and stare at it, see? Because you are perceiving the energy that is coming and going in that picture, it is a more complicated picture.

"Suppose we take the image of our Shamanic order, to freeze frame it and look at its development. If I just let the energy flow toward it, it takes different kinds of shapes. So I freeze frame it to look at it, and I say 'No, I don't want an organization.' That doesn't mean that I don't want The Eagle Tribe, but I don't want an organization. Then suddenly, it has structure to it and it becomes too complicated. I want to live simply."

*Easy Walker: Where I am, there is a fine line. When you freeze frame at the Third Eye and use the mind as a tool, how do you discern whether other stuff kicks in or you're clear?"*

"If you are at the Third Eye you are clear. You can see your own clarity by the reflection that comes back to you in the environment. If it comes back to you in chaos, you are not clear. The environment is only a mirror and it is made up of your own mind stuff.

"So yes, you produce everything yourself, including all the bogey men. They are your bogey men. So, if your husband gets upset, (looking at Wings of Change) he's also getting upset because you are throwing your bogey men into it. Here you are in companion energy and, all of a sudden, you throw a bogey man into it. (laughing) That throws everybody out of balance for a second."

*Wings of Change: "It happens because I don't feel safe within myself."*

"Well, you're getting closer and closer to that which you have to grab hold of, in order to move through the eye of the needle. That's good. It's time to put the bogey men up on the shelf so that you can see them in memory lane, in the museum. That's a childhood story."

*Wings of Change: "It's been a long term story."*

"Most childhood stories are long term for the average person, until you come to the point where you let them go. Sometime they are past life stories, but in this case, it is just a childhood story. It might have roots somewhere else though. It might have roots in another time."

# ABUNDANCE TURNED EXCESS

**Winged Wolf:** "May the blessings be.

"Whenever abundance reaches an extreme, when life becomes so abundant that you have so much, you may have the tendency to cram all kinds of activities into every nook and cranny. When you do that, the reward can only be a little bit, because you are spent up on the other side. You are overspent. It's an extravagance on the other side.

"It is important to slow down and enjoy life. Real abundance occurs when life is in balance. (Looking at Wings of Change), Your mind is so busy I can barely talk. You are overspent. So, when you tell me you can't afford to come here, I think you had no choice but to come here. It didn't make any sense anyway, did it? You have time to run in circles, to run to Europe to run here, to run there. You can afford to do all that, but you can't stand still. What is the big rush to accumulate? When you began on this path, neither one of you really knew how to make money. Then, as you began to walk the Path of Soul, you and your husband tapped into the nature of abundance and it became a game. Then it was accumulate, accumulate 'Oh, look what I can do', and that was wonderful, because that's what it was for, to learn that you could do it, that you didn't have to do without. You could have everything, do you see? But when you get caught up in it, it became an obsession.

"I'm telling you this now, because your obsessiveness holds you a prisoner. You think you're accumulating, but what you are doing is putting your body in shackles. Your life is in shackles. You have so much to take care of, just to fill a bank account, just to have things, just to multiply for multiplication's sake, which is living in excess.

"So the rewards are very minimal and you look *used up*. There is no reason you cannot have a comfortable life without being *used up*. Two Eagle's had a dream of being thrown from a car and then all of a sudden started flying. Well, it's because he went so fast he killed himself. Then he was free to fly.

"This life is a treasure. Life is a treasure. Life is a treasure! This is where it all happens, right here. That's where the multiplication happens also, but there is more to life than claiming goodies. I'm happy that you got to the stage that you don't have to worry about money. That's wonderful. I'd like to see everybody reach that stage. It's healthy. But when you become excessive, multiplying and multiplying, then you are worrying about money all the time, aren't you?. Now you are buying new businesses to have new businesses on new businesses, and you have to travel everywhere to take care of them. You are becoming a big deal, a big capitalist. You get the satisfaction of saying 'I built this', and 'I built this', but that is not enough. After awhile you will find that your body was all used up in multiplication. You won't have the health to move forward on this path. The whole point of living life is to go as far as you can, as Soul."

*Wings of Change: "How do I know when I'm crossing the line from abundance to excess?"*

"When you are obsessed with accumulation."

*Wings of Change: "I assume an obsession is similar to an addiction."*

"It is related. While listening to the raindrops today, maybe you will discover that line. This doesn't mean you should put an end to your lifestyle. It means for you to take stock of yourself, so you get what you want out of the rest of this life. You are heading for the gold ring, don't lose sight of it."

*Wings of Change: "Is it fair to ask you to not let me do that?"*

"You have to do it yourself. My not *letting* you, is bringing it forward to you right now. It's saying to you, 'I have two sage apprentices in trouble, a different kind of trouble. Everything is working so good for them, they are moving fifty million miles an hour'. I told you last year was the year of expansion. This year is the year of filling out from where you are. Otherwise you stretch the rubber band so thin, it pops, then you crash and you go off flying."

*Easy Walker: What is the difference between expansion and filling out?"*

"Well, expansion is when you are moving straight forward. Stretch it out, go as far as you can right now. When I said it is the year of expansion, I meant it's the year of expansion in each one of your lives. All life is spiritual, and I stretched those on the Path far last year. Many of you caught the wave and stretched out your businesses and your personal lives in many areas, and that is wonderful. Now, let that relax a bit so that the fullness comes back into your lives, do you see? You need to mature at this level before trying to go forward again. The maturity is very important. It is the maturity that will give you the next step. I can already sense that, as you look back at something you wanted on the spiritual path, you were saying to yourself, 'Well, maybe it's a good thing I don't have it, because I might have to give up this or that.' Now it's not that I would ask you to give up anything but refinement naturally occurs.

*Wings of Change: "That's what it looks like from the side of the fence that represents personality, not Soul?"*

"Yes, but it's the personality that becomes obsessive. Soul is not obsessive."

*"It is important to slow down and enjoy life. Real abundance occurs when life is in balance."*

# WHEN ENOUGH IS ENOUGH?

**Winged Wolf:** "When is enough, enough? When you can no longer learn from something, then step away from it. When you are doing something that is injuring you, step away from it. Stepping away, is not criticism; it is simply that in this moment of time, involvement is not useful, so you just step away.

"If someone consistently criticizes you, whether it is spoken or unspoken, how is that serving you? In what way can it serve you? It cannot serve you, and it does not serve them to do it. They are acting out of old habits, mind-sets, which they have been carrying with them since childhood. Perhaps their parents nit-picked them, and they picked it up, perpetuating it. As they grew up, they married and nit-picked their husband, and the husband finally died from it, or simply gave up wanting to live. You know, it is like, 'Enough is enough. I think I will leave here now.'

"You do not have to stay in such a situation. You do not have to die from it either, or become maimed. If a relationship is not constructive; if it does not uplift and does not serve, then there is no purpose to it. It only holds you down and makes you feel guilty for not being accepted by one you want to accept you. Being around someone who nit-picks, you develops a nit-picking attitude and, if you develop the same nit-picking attitude, you are perpetuating that which pulls you down.

"So, there comes a time to step away. There is no reason for you to be psychically murdered, and that is what it is, psychic murder. Belittling a person can actually physically and mentally maim someone.

"You have to learn to practice discrimination. If you are uplifted, as an end result, then stick with the situation. Just because times get tough, does not necessarily mean it is time to quit. Going with the flow does not mean that things are always smooth. This is a fallacy people have perpetuated in our society. 'Well, if it is tough, it means I am not supposed to go that way'. This is not so at all. Being tough sometimes may mean you have something to readjust before you can go soaring with the flow again. The rewards usually equal one's efforts.

"This is not the issue, is it? We are speaking about being nit-picked and belittled. We are speaking about people around you who use their time to study you, looking for faults. You get so that you trip over your own feet, because you feel you cannot do anything right. You may 'blow it' every time you try to do something around these people. And, it is because they are scrutinizing you so closely. Being with them is not serving you. It is not uplifting you.

"If the person is a member of your family, it doesn't mean you stop loving them, but you begin to love them in a different way. You begin to love them divinely, rather than personally. You cannot love the personal part of them, because you don't even like them, do you see? What is there to love about nit-picking? But, you can love them divinely. You can love them as Soul and respect that part of them. As you do that, you will nurture that part of them. But, you have to do it, do you see? They can't do it. You be as Soul, and as you do, it will gradually enliven Soul in them.

"I watched my own mother turn around. It was not because I tried to do anything, but because I was myself as Soul, and she became so accustomed to me being that way, it turned her around. She used to pick on other people, criticizing them, watching how they did things that did not match her way of doing things, and that was the biggest part of her criticism. The way they were doing it, did not match her mentality, not that they were doing anything wrong.

151

"One day, when she was criticizing a nurse in the nursing home. I said, 'Mother, it would be better for you if you didn't think about those people and just let them be - Better for you that you have pretty pictures in your mind. Think of the husband that you miss.' You see, ugly nit-picking pictures in your mind, and then when you die, you are going to suffer the criticism of everything you put out. It is a living hell now, and it is a living hell at death. It just goes on.

"So, use discrimination. You can do nothing to change others, but be yourself, as Soul. This does not mean that you do not fulfill your responsibilities with your parents. In the Bible it says, 'Honor thy father and thy mother', which means to care for them as they would care for you. Now, you are going to do even better than they did, because you are not going to nit-pick them. Accept them as they are. You live as Soul. Take care of their physical needs, and if you are living as Soul, they will turn around.

"Their mental machinery will become refined through your presence, because your presence as Soul will enliven Soul in them and that is the way to truly honor your mother and father. But, you never act in a certain way to try and turn them around because, if you do it for that purpose, you are manipulating them. They will know it, and, they will really pick on you for that. Refine yourself, and as you refine yourself through being as Soul, that refinement is catchy and very contagious. And, that is how you can make your world better."

*Easy Walker: "How do you discern the difference between perseverance and enough is enough?"*

"Some people will push and persevere towards a goal. They will push and persevere, push and persevere, and as they do that, their health begins to go downhill. They become unhappy, but they still push and persevere. They are operating in a mental sort of way, using their emotions to propel them. The fear of failure is propelling them. Anytime fear propels you, where are you?"

*Easy Walker: "Not as Soul!"*

"Not as Soul. And, you are suffering. Why suffer? If you are living as Soul, you do not suffer.

"Perseverance. You know, if you are on a spiritual path, or you are doing a job, do that task until it is completed, otherwise, you don't know the result. If you change from spiritual path to spiritual path, staying for just the honeymoon part in each path, the sweet nectar in the beginning of, 'Oh, this is exciting, fun and different', and move on when that starts to wear off, or when you start to refine yourself on that path, you have missed what that path is about. Walk your path. If the path dead-ends, then your teacher has dead-ended. It is time to leave. It is all that teacher can give you. Now, if you have a teacher who is truly living as Soul, the path does not ever dead-end. Life is always exciting.

"Don't miss out on what you can have. You know, this bowl of fruit is the sweetest stuff you have ever tasted and it is good for you. Enjoy the nectar of what life is about. There is so much abundance, so much fruit, so much for you to have; but, you have to claim it by going after it yourself, by doing the work."

*Easy Walker: "So, what do you do when someone nit-picks at you?"*

"If every time you look at them, you are centered at the Third Eye, you will be aware of their nit-picking, and you may choose not to be around the person for long. You don't have to hang in there to 'put your head in the garbage pail'. Why would you want to do that? Fulfill your duties and do it lovingly as Soul. Learn discrimination. Let your body be the sensor."

*Silent Feathers: You mentioned that sometimes there is a fear of failure that propels you forward. There have times where I have been more afraid of success than I have been with of failure."*

"Fear of success and fear of failure are the same thing. What do you fear in success?"

*Silent Feathers: "I fear being totally noticed and I fear being challenged in a way I do not want to be challenged."*

"So, you are afraid of failing. (Silent Feathers nods in agreement.) So, that is why I say it is the same thing.

*Silent Feathers: "Yes, there have been times when I have been afraid to say no because I felt uncomfortable. A lot of it has to do with politics and where the corporation is right now. I am realizing more and more that I do not want to be in those positions."*

"Well, it sounds to me that, if you continue going in that vein, you are going to be putting yourself out of a job. You are saying to yourself that certain things about your job are not appealing to you anymore. Well, you can say that to your employer so long, but soon you will be replaced. You see, when you make a contract to work for someone, you make a contract to do what they want. That is what they pay you for."

*Silent Feathers: "It is the politics. I cannot engage in the manipulation going on. I have even gotten up from meetings and walked out because I didn't want to be a part of what was going on.'*

"Well, your days are numbered."

*Silent Feathers: "That is okay. If that is the way it is, that is okay with me."*

"I think you would be great having your own company, a company of *one* to start. You will find a way to have your own business, and that way, you can operate it the way you want.

"Many people on the Path of Soul are self-reliant, and become self employed and they do very well at it. They are very competent. Sky Wolf, for example, is very self-reliant and self employed. He chooses who he works for. He knows how to choose what he wants that makes him feel good. He doesn't take a job just to have a job. Somebody doesn't treat him nicely, he says, 'See you later.

"Self reliance means you don't become emotionally dependent on a parent or a friend. You can share with people, but you are independent, One and whole unto yourself. And in that way, you are One and whole with everyone else."

# KARMA

**Winged Wolf:** "Sounds like we are waiting for the other shoe to drop.

"That's an interesting sound, 'waiting for the other shoe to drop', isn't it? It is a long pause while your mind waits. The shoe dropping is a karmic reaction. Hear the silence? In that silence, your mind is still, isn't it? You are listening. You are attentive to the moment. When that other shoe drops, it is your reaction to the stillness of the moment and that is the way karma works in its primary form - as a reaction to the stillness.

"In more complex life situations, karma builds complexity. First there is simplicity, the primary, the stillness. Something has to break the stillness. At this point, the karmic reaction begins and the complexity builds.

"There is a stillness that has motion to it, and that motion produces another kind of reaction. Out of that motion comes a complexity of the motion, a variance in the motion, and that variance produces a reaction that also has a variance.

"So, karma is variances of what is going on, according to the complexity of what is happening, even if nothing is happening. Out of the nothingness there will be something, because there will always be something following out of the nothingness by slight movement.

"So, there you have it. *Karma is action built upon reaction,* action followed by reaction. In life, you know that if you take an action towards anything, there will be a reaction. You can count on it. But, interestingly, if you take two similar actions, you will get two similar reactions except that they will not be exact. They will be only similar, because with each action, a motion is produced, which evolves that action the second time around, so the reaction also evolves.

"When you say to yourself, 'Well, I did it that way last time and it worked', or 'I got this result', what happens this time, is different from last time because this time there is an evolution. Today, audio taping in the Happy House with all of us gathered here together, is different from yesterday. The outcome will be slightly different today even though we are doing it the same way as we did it yesterday. It may be earmarked by Sioux's little groan in the background or whatever else will come up. Do you see?

"Your own life experiences are forever changing and forever evolving. You have heard the expression 'the only thing you can count on, is change.' This is because change is constant. More than being change, it is really an evolution of the moment, because there is only the present moment. Yesterday's moment and this moment are the same, except this moment has evolved. It is only the evolution of the moment that concerns us, not change.

"Also, within the evolution of the moment, comes a slight evolution in consciousness. That evolution in consciousness gives the appearance of change. Actually, there is no change. If you really want to know the truth, there is no such thing as change at all. It is all the same, only with a slight evolution to it, one moment to the next. This moment is no different from the preceding moment except that it has evolved, and it is your consciousness that has evolved it. This is why it is never the same when you do something a second time, a third time, or a fourth time. When you eat dinner, it is always different from the time before. When you are with your spouse making love, it is always different from the time before.

"Do not try to recapture past moments. It is impossible. You say, 'Well, my marriage used to be so wonderful'. If you are trying to reach back and recapture past moments, it will always be lived in the past. You might as well end the relationship because the relationship in the past is over.

"If you accept this present moment for whatever it is, then you have allowed the evolution of the moment, and you can be joyful in it, since living in the present moment is a very joyful experience. It does not have expectancy, except in moments of extreme quiet when you are waiting for the *shoe to drop*. You can feel it because the one thing that you know is constant, is change itself. Today we have many small interruptions. Yesterday we had none. Why can't it be like yesterday? It can't be like yesterday because yesterday was less evolved in this moment than it is now.

"Energy wants to join energy today. When your business hits a rocky time, it is a growing time. It is a time of evolution in the business. Do not look at it as something negative. Look at it as a situation that has evolved out of what was. Do you see? It has become that and in becoming that, look for the solution so that it can go around the corner and become something else. That is all it wants to do. A business in difficult straits is only an accumulation of what was. It has built to a point where it needs to turn a corner and that turning of the corner comes about very naturally through the evolution of this particular moment. But be watchful to see how to help it in this moment.

"Even *look* for solutions to motion, not through stopping the motion or intercepting this or that, but take charge without trying to control things. And you do that by recognizing that evolution of the moment is necessary for the unfoldment of the next moment. It is a healthy reaction, therefore, healthy karma.

"Now here again, I just said something, didn't I? Most people look at karma as a terrible thing. It is not at all. Action and reaction are a normal process of life. If the

158

world is falling around you, it is because of what you have done in previous moments that have accumulated and have evolved into this present moment. So, simply be still and watch the evolution. Do what you can to ease it around the corner. Clear up the mess in this way, but not through panic. Panic only produces chaos. In panic, one tries to manipulate the energy and when you try to manipulate energy, it produces chaos. You have to be careful by sitting back, watching, doing what you can, and not doing what you cannot do. Are there any questions about that?"

*Standing Turtle: "Can you plan ahead a little bit? Would that be manipulating?"*

"Making targets and goals for yourself is not manipulation. You have to take steps in preparation, but you do not do it in a panicky way.

"Sometimes you may find that you get all the way to the end of that deadline date and it still does not work out. Well, then you know that all you have gotten is an accumulation of the present moment's evolvement, in other words, the karmic reaction. That is just the way it is. Perhaps you have not seen that it could have gone in another way that is actually going to give you a result that will better benefit the situation. This is because you set the whole process of evolution into motion, so by the time you get down to the other end of the track, it is really going the way you set it in motion.

"Maybe it was an oversight back there. Maybe you settled for something else because you got tired or busy or whatever. You can count on the fact that whatever you buried previously, will show up down the line, therefore anytime you think you are avoiding something, you might as well give up that idea. The karmic reaction of avoidance is bringing something into the foreground, so drag your feet and procrastinate all you like, you will get a double whammy from it every single time.

"There is no point in trying to sweep something under the rug, thinking that it will go unnoticed. It does not go unnoticed! You can play all the little games you want but it is still there and it will come forward. Whether another person brings it forward deliberately is not important. It is all part of the evolutionary process of karma. What comes around goes around. You can count on it. You reap what you sow. People say, 'I did all this for so and so and look at the way they are treating me'. Well, you did all that for so and so with a desired result. That is manipulation which creates chaos. You see, you caused the result, yourself.

"Manipulation does not bring about desired results. Although it may seem that way in the beginning, during the actual manipulation, sooner or later it will backfire. The true evolutionary process will reveal itself and the karmic reaction will be there. If it was manipulation, it will turn into the chaos of the other person not performing the way you wanted. Every situation will have an outcome!

"Now, if you made a mistake somewhere along the line by being too tired or too disinterested in taking care of a detail, that detail will naturally surface through the evolutionary process of karma. But since you did not actually manipulate that detail, it will have a lesser impact when it comes back. Do not deliberately ignore something, because if you do, you will have chaos through your own manipulation.

"Sometimes life goes so fast and you are so busy that you see something you are going to take care of, but you get caught up in other things and miss it. It will come back to you, never-the-less. The karmic reaction will happen. Although the impact of the karmic reaction will not be as severe, you will still have to deal with it."

*Standing Turtle: "How can past life karma be dealt with without getting into despair after you start to recognize it?"*

"When you have a fear that is totally out of context with the moment and you cannot honestly say that it had anything to do with the previous moments in this life, it has to do with previous moments in a past life. The past life and this life are really the same, except you are wearing a slightly different suit of clothing. Your form is slightly different because it evolved as well. Your form is a karma, do you see? You wear the body that you evolved to be.

"Everything that you have strong feelings about that you cannot relate to the rest of your life, comes from a past existence. I knew that when I was a child, I had a terrible fear of bridges. I can remember my parents driving the car across the Chesapeake Bay bridge, which is about five miles long, and I was terrified. That fearful experience had nothing to do with this lifetime. Nobody could ever understand it, but I dealt with it, because even as a fourteen year old girl, I realized that, if I didn't deal with it, it was going to ruin my life. One day I went out to this little country bridge in Virginia where I grew up. I sat down on the bridge and I cried and cried and shivered and shook. Then, I made friends with the bridge all by myself. Anybody who has a fear of heights or fear of sickness or a fear of whatever, make friends with it. *Make friends with your fear so that the energy that holds you spellbound in that fear no longer controls you.*

"Do not let somebody else try to do this for you. If my parents had tried to get me to make friends with the bridge, I would have been terrified with resentment."
*Two Eagles: "You said earlier if you were sitting in the silence there will be a karmic reaction, so it sounds like karma is a motivating force in the cycle somehow."*

"Karma is both the movement of the cycle and the reaction of the cycle. It is the result of the movement. The movement itself is the energy, so it is the result of the movement of energy."

*Standing Turtle: "Is that like perpetual motion? It is said that some kids are always in perpetual motion."*

"All energy is in perpetual motion because all energy is the energy of the Void. The Void is always evolving because of that perpetual motion. You and I are continually evolving because *you and I are the Void*. We carry the Void energy. Our bodies are the Void manifest."

*Standing Turtle: "Is the consciousness that we are aware of, as we become aware of the consciousness of Soul, a part of our karma?"*

"When karma from the past gets cleared up, you still have your present moment karma. The karma from your past lives is cleared up when you attain Shaman Consciousness. There is nothing binding you. You feel as though you are living another lifetime.

"Your karma will be cleared up, giving you a fresh start. Since you are living wholeheartedly in the present, you must not sweep any present day situation under the rug. Simply deal with what comes up now, in the present moment. When I had a boundary problem with my neighbor, I handled it immediately when I first moved here, though I would have preferred to have turned my head and looked away. If I had ignored the problem, I would still be dealing with it now. It is always more difficult to deal with old karma than it is with present karma. So, when something comes up, deal with it immediately by staying in the moment.

"Now there is proper timing. You have to wait for it to actually confront you. You don't go out looking in anticipation of what could happen. If you do, you are not living in the moment. You are manipulating. When you deal with situations as they come up, that is non-manipulative and you will erase any negative karma as you are doing it. On the other hand, if you say, 'Oh! I don't want to deal with that now', believe me, you will deal with it in a bigger package as it accumulates. It is like a snowball that builds and builds until it is too heavy to deal with. For this reason, do not let things accumulate.

"This is like people who accumulate debt. Soon it becomes an overwhelming burden. In our society, a little debt is okay to meet your needs but always keep a handle on what you are doing. Do not let things get out of hand. When you put something on your credit card, know how you are going to deal with it. Do not get yourself trapped. Do not let anybody talk you into getting trapped, because you are not only trapped by what they talked you into karmically, but you are trapped by the act of allowing yourself to be talked into a situation.

"Life does not have to be complicated. It can be simple, clear cut and fun, without hassle, by keeping it clean in the moment, by keeping the moment clean. Do what you have to do in this moment.

"Procrastinators never have enough of anything because they have not dealt with the moment. I have compassion for them, but not sympathy. Compassion has nothing to do with sympathy. Procrastinators make karma out of their procrastination for themselves.

"People who procrastinate in one area, usually procrastinate in all areas. Usually, they are schemers and manipulators because they have to scheme their way out of situations they failed to carry through. It is not a very honorable way to live."

# RESOLVING KARMA

**Winged Wolf:** "The other day we spoke about karma and what it is. Now, let us take a look at how to get rid of it. Of course, we want to hang onto the karma that is going to serve us in life, that which is good, which creates little windfalls of happiness, bounty, abundance, and joy.

"But most people have had a set way of living through the years. They have developed attitudes and opinions about themselves, about the world, about their families, and about their friends - and they project all this into the world.

"When you feel irritable in a person's presence, it is because they are carrying anger karma. When people are difficult to be around, you feel like you cannot look at them, or speak to them, and you maybe don't know why. Well, it is because of the anger that they carry inside of them.

"Anger is not always expressed as an open rage. Sometimes it is an inner rage that lives in one's body, in the forms of frustration, guilt, feelings of not being as good as somebody else, inadequacies, or maybe a feeling that the world owes them something and they didn't get their proper share. For instance, they may say, 'Why am I born with these circumstances?' When we come in contact with them our eyes look away, or we get busy, unconsciously avoiding their presence. We don't care to talk to them or have any activity with them, although sometimes there are certain periods where we feel okay in their presence, as well. This usually occurs when they are feeling strong, confident and relaxed.

"Well, all these effects may seem like little things but they are lodged in the memory bodies of those you have touched in your life. They are lodged in the nature of situations you have lived through, and those situations often involve other people. They also involve animals, plants, insects, and all kinds of things. Insects are sentient beings, as well.

"So, the general environment has an awareness of sorts, about feelings you hold inside, by what you project, and all of that is lodged in their memory, even without them even being conscious of it. You may have projected a specific nature or tone to situations while in participation with them, and that tone still lives in your relationships. It may continue for years, until, gradually, life brings it to your attention. You begin to see it because your karmic relationships block you from going further on the path.

"When you recognize the blockage, there is a natural desire to conquer the life-long difficulty. First, you resolve to stop it. But, what happens when you resolve to stop it? There is a backlash. All of a sudden everything starts coming at you. 'What's this? I'm having this problem and this problem and this problem'. Well, you are paying your dues. All of a sudden, circumstances in the environment are doing to you that you used to do, even though you are not doing it anymore. Do you see? 'I'm not doing that anymore. Why is it picking on me?' Well, it is still lodged in the ethers out there. Everything you put out there is lodged out there. It is similar to stretching a rubber band. When you let go of it, 'whap' it goes right back in your face.

"However, there is a way out of this kind of karma. You do not have to live the rest of your life in misery, catching up for the forty years that you have already lived, because that is what it would take to work it out, another forty years to clear up everything you have put out for forty years; an equal amount of time!

"The way out, is through Soul Vision. Now, when I say Soul Vision, I mean living at the Third Eye, which means *living one hundred percent in the present moment.*

165

If, for one instant, you allow yourself to slip from the present moment consciousness, you get that backlash coming at you again. This is a good incentive to Live As Soul!

"Every time you fall out of Soul Vision, the backlash is going to happen, *even* when you sleep at night and you fall into old dream patterns. You may have a nightmare, or you may wake up with an attitude and immediately, the backlash will hit you.

"Somewhere in the Bible it says, 'Put your hands to the plow and never look back'. That is what this means. You have your attention looking forward, looking at the bullseye, living exactly in the present moment. You are at the plow. You have your attention where you are directing that plow. You must never look back to see what you have done. If you look back, the backlash is going to get you, because you are not in the present moment.

"You must live in the present moment, whole-heartedly. The only way you can stay in the present moment is to be wholehearted; and wholeheartedness is impeccability itself. When you are wholehearted, you cannot wander off the Path.

"Strive to be impeccable. Use discrimination. It is necessary to make a clear choice about what you are deciding to do, otherwise, you are going to make choices that create chaos. 'Here I am wholeheartedly in the present moment, but I'm making a choice that's going to throw me right back into chaos.' What a horrible result. Do you see? You can't stay in that present moment because you are always allowing yourself to be pulled out of it. This is where the teacher comes in. You have to use your teacher, if you have one.

"You can use your teacher to help you stay focused in the moment. This does not mean you always pick up the telephone to speak to your teacher. There is already a string of energy connecting you and your teacher. This next point is important, so please pay attention. Your teacher, if you have one, must be a "physical" teacher. It cannot be a teacher who died five hundred years ago or even a year ago. It has to be a teacher who is alive in a physical body, so you can draw on those physical strings of energy in emergencies. Remember though, that no real teacher is going to let you use them as a crutch. You have to do the work yourself, but you can call on that reserve.

"As long as you are truly present in the moment and you are sincerely trying to find your way out of a predicament, the teacher will step in and guide you so that you can learn discrimination for yourself and see beyond your myth for yourself.

"Now, there is a price to pay, a great big price. Your teacher will demand your impeccability, your wholehearted impeccability. You give any less than that and your teacher is going to turn away.

"You have to toe the line. 'Well, that means an authority figure. I don't like authority figures.' Well, so what? Remember, in your own lives you are an authority figure to someone, to your children, or at work. It is a part of life. At least in this instance, you have decided to do it, and never forget that. It is your choice."

*Gazelle: "Is karma and our myth the same?"*

"You fashioned your myth through your attitudes, opinions and ideas about yourself and society. Much of it is all fantasy.
"Through fantasy, people project life. Everything they do, they do with fantasy propelling them. It can make a big mess, which is why a teacher is needed. They have been looking at life through fantasy glasses for so long, it has become commonplace. They cannot see themselves."

*Two Eagles: "So, without the teacher you cannot distinguish between the facsimile memory versus the real memory?"*

"You may get a little glimmer of distinction, but to break its hold on you and move in another direction, you require a guide, which is what a teacher is. Resolving karma cannot be accomplished by simply looking at past situations and chewing on them, like you would do in a therapeutic situation. Do you see? Resolving karma has nothing to do with chewing on old situations.

"Many times you had a memory of something, and couldn't tolerate the outcome of it. It didn't suit you, do you see? Something happened and you didn't like it, so you changed the outcome. You changed the outcome of the story about the incident to suit yourself. This is not bad in some cases. In some cases, where you have the opportunity to make lemonade out of lemons, changing the story may have served you.

"But, what does not serve you, is your unconscious that you did it, or your refusal to admit to yourself that you did it. The situation then becomes shady and you develop an attitude.

"You do not need to go back and unravel the past. When you try to do that, you perpetuate new fantasies. You try to go back to unravel the past, because you cannot remember exactly, or it does not feel right to remember exactly, so you make a fantasy about what you remember. Then you are creating more karma for yourself.

"You cannot resolve karma by chewing over the past. If something bad happened to you, say, 'Oops! Something bad happened to me in the past. It is over now.' Keep your attention on the present moment and do not go back on it. The more you chew on a past situation, remembering with emotion, the more your fantasy gets locked in there. The more you chew on it, the more alive it becomes and the more embellished it becomes. You see? It takes on flesh and bones and becomes real. You know, if you were raped as a child, your fearful memory compounds it up into something worse and you carry it around with you as you live your life."

*Two Eagles: "This whole thing about recovered memories and, supposedly what somebody remembers from childhood about some terrible thing that happened, is that a valid issue?"*

"Much is stimulated through the person who is trying to help someone remember the past issue. I am not saying that some people have not had a rough road to hoe. I have many apprentices who have had really horrible childhoods. Many of them have also had nice childhoods. There are some ugly stories out there, but in the nicer stories everyone likes to think, 'Well I had it rough too'. It is getting complicated in the world today. Couples with children are almost afraid to clean their children's bottoms! You know, they fear being labeled sexual abusers. They are thinking to themselves, 'Am I molesting my child'. For heaven sakes, there is so much focus on misery, debauchery, and sexual sicknesses, that people are becoming mentally sick. Garbage pail consciousness.

*Two Eagles: "Is the mass consciousness taking on that fantasy?"*

"Absolutely. You see it on television. People are perpetuating what they fear. 'Well, maybe something happened to me as a kid. I remember I had an uncle that looked at me funny one time. Let's see, did he do something?' So what? *Leave it alone. Look at now. Live as Soul now.* Develop your life now. What the heck does going back and living in the past do? It compounds karma, and not happy karma, negative karma! Living in the present moment presents happy karma in your life. It presents happy karma, because of what you are giving to life while living in the present moment. You are so wholehearted, happy, and joyful, filled with expanding this moment so much that you just automatically slip into the next moment. When life is exciting, exuberating, and fun, that then, is the karma that is perpetuated."

*Standing Turtle: "We have compassion for those who have been abused, but what about the perpetrators? What about their karma?"*

"Why don't you leave them alone and not pass judgment on them. The person who did you wrong, did you wrong; that is something they have to live with. That is something they have to sort out. If you try to live everybody's karma and everybody's situation, you are going to get angry at them, because you are passing judgment on them. 'Oh, they are bad. They should never have done this. They should never have done that.' That person should be thrown in jail. Oh, so and so just married so and so and 'Oh, they are really asking for it. This person is terrible. Blah. Blah'. Allow each other to change and grow. Do not put each other into molds.

"When you judge another person, you are living in that person's consciousness. When you get angry at someone, you mentally associate with their actions, which means you live in their state of consciousness. Consequently, you give your power to them. *Don't do that!* Do not give your power away to somebody who did you in. Do you see? Instead, learn Soul Vision. It makes life current, and alive, *passionate in the moment.*

"When you are feeling angry at someone, you actually step into that other person's consciousness. You are taking on the same sickness they had and they may not even have it any more. They may have grown beyond

170

and evolved and changed their whole life and who knows, maybe they are working with a shaman teacher.

"They may have already faced that problem and moved on, but you are still there looking back at it. You are living where they were living, while you are trying to move on. That is like standing on your own foot so you cannot walk."

Two Eagles: "There is a powerful myth about being in other people's business."

"Well, it is boredom with your own life, isn't it? If you are in the present moment, there is no boredom. Living as Soul there is passion for everything you do wholeheartedly. You feel the blood rushing through your veins. Life is exciting. The minute you think you have to get out there and live somebody else's life, you are stepping into their karma. You are not resolving your own karma, you are stepping into theirs. You take this block of their karma and you bring it into your life. And you wonder why you have so many problems. Not only are you living your karma from the past, you are living somebody else's karma in the present! What a mess!

"As Soul, you will learn what true aliveness is. I am talking about being alive versus talking about existing in life, surviving in life, which is very low on the survival scale. I live at the top of the survival scale. That is, I live by choice in the present moment. Being at the top of the survival scale is the gift of living in the present moment as Soul."

# EARTH CHANGES...

## and the Healing of Our Breathing Earth Mother

**Winged Wolf:** "I went into the kitchen early one morning to make a cup of tea when, suddenly, I let out a forceful sneeze. The cat jumped off the kitchen counter, and the pots and pans that were hanging above my head, suddenly clanged together. I glanced up at dangling pots and pans, which were quickly settling into their normal repose. They seemed high enough above me not to be affected by the sneeze. Then I had the opportunity to re-test the hypothesis. I sneezed again. As before, the vibration of my "ahh-choo" set the pans chiming. I looked around the kitchen. The cat was gone. Sioux approached from in front of the refrigerator where she had been watching me in curious wolf expression to poke me in the thigh with the end of her nose.

"*All that commotion for a sneeze! Do you get my point? Please pay careful attention.*

"Everyone talks about the law of cause and effect but few take responsibility for the causes they make. You know, and I know, that what is put into something must come out in some way. The vibration of a sneeze affected the environment in my kitchen and set the dangling pans in motion. The pans ingested the vibration and reacted by releasing it. Release is a healthy follow-up for reaction. It is a letting go of something once held or reacted to. This principal is at work in every area of our lives. If all the food we ever ate collected in our bodies, we would explode. Likewise, if all the feelings we ever felt went unexpressed, or untransmuted, we would become miserable, sick, and gradually die from depression.

"The Earth, like ourselves, is a living organism. The earth's affectations are similar to those of human mannerisms in that the earth displays what it feels through reaction. An earthquake is a reaction from the building up of pressure beneath the surface of the earth. Thus, the reaction of an earthquake to pressure, releases or relieves the underground strain of shifting rock. The earthquake can compound itself in the form of a tidal wave. Tidal waves are formed by excessively strong winds, which science has defined as "widespread movement, or strong feeling."

"The very fact that we humans present "widespread movement, or strong feeling," as explanations of scientific relationships about the forces of nature, suggests that we recognize the inherent domination of humans over biological existence. In a nutshell, I am saying, all life is Soul. Soul is a part of God. The earth and its trees and bushes, animals and insects; the oceans and rivers and rainfall, and fishes; birds, the air and the combustion of it, fire, are all Soul and, as such, have consciousness. The difference between Soul as a human being and Soul as other forms of organic life, is that the human is aware of its consciousness. In other words, nature feels its creatures "know," but humanity "knows it knows." This being true, humanity dominates organic life through conscious intelligence.

"Recently, I was sitting in the living room of my home chatting with a visiting apprentice. Alan listened to what I had to say and then counterpointed with a feeling of his own. As he thrust his viewpoint at me, his knee jumped nervously up and down, and wood floors and walls seemed to move with him. As he was talking in this way, he suddenly became aware of himself and the movement he was causing to happen in the living room. "Did I make this room move or what?" he asked, astonished at himself. "You made it move," I answered in

173

agreement. "An earth-shaking argument," he remarked, laughing. "Almost," I added.

"It is an architectural fact that a specific number of people marching in unison can cause a bridge to sway and even to collapse.

"This is important! As sensible people, we know eating rotten food will make us sick, and yet we ingest poison. For years, agricultural workers have sprayed poisons on our crops. The leafy vegetables are fed chlorophyll to appear green and healthy. Fruits are sometimes dyed and frequently waxed to make them more appealing. Animals that are raised for food are fed steroids and other poisonous chemicals for greater bulk, and yet we are shocked that anemia and cancer have become common words in our society.

"People look for causes, but they don't want to change their lifestyles. If one person carries anger inside of themselves, their life will, in some way, depict that anger. If a thousand people carry anger inside of themselves, living a near-violent, stressful existence, then that much anger is presented outwardly into the world. If an entire society suffers, an entire society is affected and the societies of other countries are affected. In likeness, the earth and the atmosphere are both affected.

"The most common concern by people are land mass changes and the predictions of doom. Science has read the signs of our times. Religions are geared up to call in the "straying flock." "It will only get worse," they tell us. Those who live on the coast, where earthquakes are more likely, are moving inland to Arizona and Colorado. What they don't realize is that, if California and New York are devastated, the effects will be felt far in the middle states. The land will shift everywhere. Even the Rocky Mountains will sink a thousand or so feet. Arizona may turn into a seaport, but thousands upon thousands of lives, and thousands of acres of land, will be lost in the shuffle. The midwest may have the most stable land, but continuously changing air currents will produce constant tornadoes. The magnetic poles of the earth will shift and the weather will drastically change in every section of the country.

"So why worry about moving to safety? Where will you go? People will be running like chickens in a barnyard trying to escape a fox.

"There is a way out of all of this. The earth mother is a living, breathing organism. She is sick, but she can be healed. The first thing we can do is to stop talking about the devastation that doomsdayers predict. Fear produces disease in an individual and in all organic life. Constant worry over something enlarges the area of concern. Worry produces more of what you are worried about. Instead, we should place our attention on solutions. We must put fear aside and take action to produce health individually, and in our environment.

"Mother Earth can be healed by forward positive feelings. We need to stop *feeling* that the worst is about to happen and be joyful instead. Being joyful comes from living impeccably, or aligning our actions with our dreams, which means we must BE HONEST with ourselves and live accordingly. No longer can we afford to live as a sick society would have us live. We must heal our society, and we do so by centering ourselves at the "Third Eye" area in the center of our foreheads, at the seat of Soul. When we do this, we find that we no longer escape from a stressful life by absorbing violent action movies into our consciousness, or any other form of inharmonious living. We will want to make changes in our mental and physical diet. We can choose healthier foods and uplifting entertainment. We can live according to our TRUE heart's desire, thus transmuting the ill health of ourselves and the breathing earth, to a radiance of well-being."

# THE NATURE OF POWER

**Winged Wolf:** "Power" is a word that catches everyone's attention. Say the word aloud in a crowded room and heads turn to face the speaker. It is as if the speaker is the power itself for daring to call out the name, for that is what the word "power" is, a name, and a name is the primary symbol to call forth the energy it implies. Naturally, with potency that dramatic, power is something that most everyone would like to possess for some purpose or another.

"Power means many things to many different people, but generally speaking, when people think of power, they think of a forceful energy that has the steam to accomplish a goal. It is synonymous with success. The goal can be a love relationship, money, stature in the community, or job related. How this energy is interpreted depends on the interpreter and how they view life, and this is where people get into difficulty.

"Each individual views life through their own experience, and/or heresay experience, which are the experiences of others, and the conclusions these others have reached. Most heresay experience comes from family, friends, television and movies, whereas personal experience is concluded by a participant's actual actions and reactions. When things work out positively, power is considered "good." When they work out poorly, power is viewed as "bad." What many people forget, or do not realize, is that power is neither good or bad. Power is energy and it lives in the neutral zone. It is the use of power that determines its effects.

"When a person plots or creates a scenario involving other people to bring about a certain result, they are using energy to manipulate a reaction. Reaction, "good" or "bad", is born out of conflict. Conflict, either visible or invisible, forms within one's personal environment at the exact moment an individual begins to manipulate energy.

"Anytime energy is used to manipulate a reaction, there will be consequences, and these consequences will either be felt as "good" or "bad." You can depend on it. Manipulation of any kind demands reaction or payment, which reverts back to the manipulator in the form of responsibility. And there are no "free rides." The law of action/reaction is very exacting on the manipulative level and when retribution time occurs, the consequences cannot be ducked.

"This is how people become awed by the name POWER. Those who have placed their hand on this hot stove, have felt the sting of their manipulation. Since they know of no other way, they become afraid of power, afraid of success, afraid of failure. Those who have acquired the "touch" to keep the energies at bay, and have created success through chaos, may argue that their manipulations of the energy have "payed off."

"The payoff" is the lure of the manipulative power. That is how manipulative power works.

"Sometimes one can go along for a period of time, manipulating this and that - people and things - and everything seems to happen just as planned. Then suddenly, the tide changes. What was "paying off" turns sour, and usually with the same fervor that the manipulation was applied. There is a backlash of energy that usually keeps up for however long the manipulation occurred. This is natural law, which is also psychic law, and there is no way around it. The cycle works its way up to the top of the wave, to a point of success through manipulation, and then things go downhill. Unfortunately, manipulative situations usually have to hit bottom before a new cycle begins. There is, however, a way out, a way to live on top of the wave, to so-called "Have your cake and eat it too.

"The nature of power to a Shaman is to live as Soul, with one's attention on the Third Eye, or in Soul Vision. Here the energy-producing power, lives freely in the individual, so that everything that is required, is provided. In this state, the internal dialogue is cut off and the mind is quiet. Since one's mind is not cluttered with plots and manipulative plans, the individual is mentally brilliant, joyful, and at peace, living in heightened awareness. There is no longer any conflicting thought to block success. Arriving at this state is a process, but not necessarily a long process. As my teacher Alana Spirit Changer said to me, "Shamanism means to live in ecstasy, however, sometimes we must rearrange ourselves to live there."

# THE HEALING POWERS OF SOUL

**Winged Wolf:** "Did you learn today what 'May the Blessings Be' means? Did you experience it? It means, the flood gates are being opened. (Looks around at those in attendance.)

"Tonight's talk is, 'The Healing Powers of Soul'. I am sure that each of you experienced some of that today. I heard tales of the healing power, here and there. As you are learning Soul Vision, an interesting thing happens. It begins as a second here or a few seconds there, and then another minute or another half minute somewhere else. Maybe in the beginning you can sustain Soul Vision five whole minutes in the day consciously. And you begin to experiment with it more, because you get an inkling of something going on, even though you are not quite sure what. So the next day and the days after that, you continue to practice. Your practice brings you to a point where you can sustain Soul Vision a couple of minutes at a time, maybe even five or ten minutes, and the length of time continues.

"Pretty soon, throughout the day, you can reach a half hour to forty-five minutes, or maybe even an hour throughout the day in conscious Soul Vision. As you do this, something begins to happen to your body and to your life.

"Within your brain there are nerve endings that overlap. Throughout a busy day, these nerve endings often tense up, and actually knit together forming a knot. But now that you are being in Soul Vision a half hour, forty-five minutes to an hour a day, that tension begins to relax. Areas of the brain you never used before start to come alive.

"Areas of the brain are tense, produce headaches and nervousness. These areas relax when you are in Soul Vision, but every time you have a doubt in your life, or you become frightened, or when your emotions flare up, there forms another glitch in your brain.

"Once you can sustain Soul Vision for a half hour, forty-five minutes or an hour throughout the entire day, those nerve centers begin to relax. Euphoric moments, when you feel perfectly clear, occur when the brain is relaxed. When you become tense, they tighten again. After awhile, you get so that you recognize when the opening and closing occurs in your brain and then, something else occurs. Parts of your brain, which were previously unfamiliar to you, begin to awaken. Abilities and talents that have been latent, begin to open up. The body begins to glow. You begin to glow like a person in love.

"When you live as Soul in Soul Vision, a glow appears on your skin. There is a light coming from you and that light does things. First of all, the light is attractive and it attracts beauty into your life, because you are feeling the beauty. Soul Vision produces health in one's body, and there is harmony.

"Something else occurs around the time you begin to glow. Your capability of staying in Soul vision is extended longer and longer and longer, and parts of your brain previously unused come alive.

"You know, scientists tell us that we use about five percent of our brains, a number which enlarges in Soul Vision. As Soul, one's brain begins to enliven itself. It has no conflict. It heals not only the body, but the brain.

"So other areas of your life, also, become healed. Your finances become more balanced. Your marriage becomes harmonious. Your family worries are resolved, all because you are carrying Soul aliveness in you.

"Your intellect sharpens. Your IQ literally jumps 30 to 40 points, maybe more. You can now use knowledge belts available to you and you can do things that you could never do before, because you have no conflict going on within the brain to intercept what you want to do.

"To fear Soul Vision is pure insanity. You develop capabilities through living as Soul that you never had before. I don't know its limitations. I don't feel that there are any. I am always moving forward like you are. Everyday I learn something new about Soul Vision. Everyday I experience something new as Soul.

"When your mind begins to argue with you, telling you to be afraid of these changes, or, you hear yourself saying, 'I feel like I'm losing my mind', that means the mind is quieting down and, suddenly, it looks at itself and it says, 'It's too quiet in here. I'm not used to this. Where is the mind chatter?' It is the 'habit' of a chattering mind, rehashing things, mulling over, every little thing that is missing.

"Allow the quiet to occur. It is okay for the mind to argue. Let it. Don't try to stop it. Don't argue or fight it. Don't treat the mind as an enemy. It is your best friend! It is the best tool you have, when functioning properly. Soul Vision, remember, is not the tool, it is a way of life. The mind is the tool.

"Now, because you are now practicing Soul Vision *consciously*, three or four hours a day, you are becoming a very brilliant person, brilliant in your flesh and brilliant in your brain. You might begin to learn to draw and paint, even if you never could before. You might find all kinds of hidden talents within you. You have a new sense of freedom and you can try anything you want to try, because there is no conflict inside saying, 'But what of this? But what of that?' *You are free to enjoy life!*

"There is a richness about life in Soul Vision that is wonderful. There is abundance that there was never before. Your business begins to multiply, because you do not waste energy in conflict or worry. Worrying is the most

181

useless thing we can do. It takes a tremendous amount of energy. It promotes tension within the brain and it short circuits whatever it is that you are trying to do. You are going in one direction and you are thinking another thing - conflict.

"As Soul, when you are living in Soul Vision, you are looking out of yourself. You are seeing the world as it is, so your choices are clear. You are not confused. You know what you want, and you reach out to get it. When you do something, there is no wasted energy.

"You become a brilliant mental giant, as well as a brilliant loving human being. If you've had a mental block about mathematics all your life, you'll probably open up a book on calculus and understand it.

"Things you used to have mental blocks about, in childhood or adulthood; now, seems perfectly clear. It wasn't so difficult after all. The difficulty came from all those glitches in your brain, short circuiting your intelligence.

"The Healing Powers of Soul: We've learned that healing means to heal an entire life, not the physical body alone. People with cancer can heal themselves with proper nutrition and by living as Soul. We have apprentices who have done that.

"Never fall short on your practice of Soul Vision. You want it to be a way of life, not a tool. Don't ever get that confused. Live it! Carry it with you! Talk to your friends while looking out of yourself! See what is around you!

"When you are speaking to people, rather than trying to think in words inside of your mind, look and allow your body to direct you through feeling, to perceive the energy there. Our bodies are instruments. They are not only vehicles for us to walk around from place to place, to take us somewhere, they are sensory objects that help us perceive energy in another person, or in a place. We walk into a room and we can feel the energy of that place and it feels comfortable or uncomfortable, but you can only really know that in Soul Vision. If you try to feel, using your mind as a guide, you will become confused. 'Well, it felt this way, but I'm not sure. It could be this or this.' You won't make any of those mistakes if you are in Soul Vision. I guarantee it.

"Your business judgment will be sound. Your family judgment will be sound. Your judgment on health will be sound. You will be able to see what you need to do to take care of yourself. And, as Soul, those little nerve endings begin to relax so even cancer reverses itself.

"Now what we are saying sounds very simplistic, but it is not. It is very, very difficult. It is very simple but it is very difficult. It is difficult because you carry a myth and that is what you have been living life through, the myth, the fantasy.

"Looking at life through fantasy, you are unable to see where you are going, so, you cannot stay in Soul Vision. Your myth keeps you from doing it. That's the part changing now. You are beginning to live it. Some of you are further along than others, so, if you see somebody get in trouble or stumble and fall, have compassion. As Soul, there is always compassion, never judgment.

"Pick yourself up if you fall. Dust yourself off and go on. The more you can practice Soul Vision, the freer you will become, the healthier you will become, the happier you will become, the more alive, the more intelligent, the more brilliant in every way. You will be able to experience life to its fullest in a healthy, happy state.

"One of the best things that you can do for yourself when you are having trouble staying in Soul Vision is to laugh. We did that today. It also helps to walk and swing your arms at your sides so that your back muscles can relax. Then you can free your body up so it can be 'tuned in' again and you can get back into Soul Vision.

"Remember, the seat of Soul in the body, this third eye in the center of your forehead, is a physical part of the body. We focus on it to bring ourselves into that state of heightened awareness. You have to be relaxed. You have to find your comfort zone. Physical exercise is very, very important every single day. Walking is the best. It is the best, because you are walking through scenery, whatever the scenery may be. You are swinging your arms. Your body is in motion. Your whole body is in motion. Motion, doing, is very, very important."

*"Don't treat the mind as an enemy. It is your best friend. It is the best tool that you have. Soul Vision, remember, is not the tool; it is the way of life. The mind is the tool."*

# MEMORY

**Winged Wolf:** "Everybody knows that memory follows you throughout your day, the little things that were done a half hour ago, yesterday, or even years ago. Something will push a button and remind you of something that happened when you were young.

"Sometimes there are memories that are like icons or images in your life that are not connected to anything and they have little meaning to you. They are subtle images that you thought about as a child because the memories that you looked at then were mere play things.

"As you grew older, you saw your childhood images occasionally because they had been around so long. They were so much a part of everything that, when you looked at them, you paid no attention, because they were just there. In fact, they have *always* been there, as long as you can remember.

"Very deep into the waking up process, something happens one day. An image of that icon appears as it always did, but this time you are prepared to see it for the first time. You say to yourself 'Yes, I see that".

"Let's say the image is an elephant. (It doesn't have to be an elephant, it could be a rock, a shovel, a symbol of something.) This elephant picture is just there. It is something that is subtle. This does not mean that you like to go to the zoo and look at elephants, although that might be a point of fascination when you do. This has no connection to your present life. You don't feel anything from it. It is just an image that flashes before your inner eyes. Now you are at the zoo and the elephant is standing there in front of you. You look at it without the memory that it has been an icon throughout your life. There is no memory at all.

"When you leave the zoo you forget about it. Maybe five, ten, or even thirty years pass and all of a sudden there it is again, the image of the elephant. You have seen it many times in the past but have never paid attention to it. Only this time, when you see it, it is like striking the chord of an instrument. It makes a dramatic impact on you.

"Perhaps this happens in the middle of the night. What! The Elephant. You are staring at the elephant again. What is this elephant? For the first time you wake up in the night and you really look at this elephant in awareness, not full awareness, but awareness that the elephant has some strong meaning and has left images throughout your life. Now they come back to you.

"All of a sudden you remember a time that had nothing to do with this lifetime. You remember when the elephant was a symbol to you in some special way. You do not remember all the details of everything that occurred, but you might remember a word you used to say when you were a child, a made-up word that now connects to the memory of the elephant.

"Children up until four years of age remember many things, so this word was said in a slightly funny way, because you were a child. You remember the image was not 'fuzzy wig' or 'chessiewig', instead the word might have been connected to a past experience. The words 'fuzzy wig' that you used to say as a little child when said in proper language, was 'Ganesha', a symbolic deity of enlightenment which the elephant is in India. Do you see? The image or icon does not have to be the elephant. Whatever it is, it is something connected to this moment in a past life that makes images come clear.

"When do those images come to you? When are they clear? It would depend on what the image was about and your readiness to receive that image. If in the past, there was a rock on which you always stood at the edge

186

of a cliff or a jetty to see a waiting boat, then throughout your life, you might have been looking at rocky scenery, never truly connecting it, until one day that image appears, and all the images that you have ever had of it come together to give you the image of where it originated. It comes when you are ready to receive it, or when it is important in your life for you to receive it.

"'When it is important' means that it is entering your life again. It is a seed you brought into this life from a past life because it is karmically attached to you. That lookout jetty is karmically attached to you and, as you remember it, you will remember scenes of it. You will remember what happened and you will remember the karma. This does not mean that you will go to live by the sea again, but you may.

"At this point, you have accessed the Akashic Records with your memory, because your karma of that past moment is coming to fruition in this moment, so pay attention. It may not happen for a long time and this doesn't matter. If you intentionally look for it, you will never find it because it is too subtle. You see it but your awareness will not attach to it yet. You have to wait until your awareness is ripe. When you discover that karmic tie to this lifetime, you will remember all pertinent ties from all lifetimes. You will know who you have been in the past that has made you who you are in the present. What you will remember will not be incidents necessarily, but you will remember bits and pieces of that karmic tie and will perceive the karma through the energy of living as Soul.

"Karma is not good or bad. It just is. Without karma you would not come back to life. It is a point of earning. It represents your bank account. It is what you have stored up. It is all the coins in the basket and now you can see them for the first time. What a dramatic impact it is. Now, because you see your karma so fully, most likely your karmic deeds of the past are wiped away. The past is no longer there, except as you live in the present in your awareness. Your awareness is greatly heightened at this time and can be anywhere from greatly heightened to total awareness, depending on the karmic debt that you carried forward.

"This is when you step into your freedom. Your freedom says that the limitlessness of living is the same as the limitlessness of dying. I just wanted to share that with you. It is so quietly subtle. These little icons or images that come up from the past are a quiet gift we humans carry within ourselves. There is a reason in mentioning things like this because, when it is mentioned, it wakes up a section of your brain and you become more conscious. A block that was there, that was just a subtle image sitting in front of you, now takes shape. Do not look for it. Do not ever look for it. Just watch and see what comes."

# PRACTICING THE HU

**Winged Wolf:** "May the blessings be."

Taking a shoe string from one of Standing Turtle's shoes to use as an illustration, Winged Wolf began working with Sky Wolf on the sounds of the HU. (Sky Wolf is deaf). Winged Wolf held one end of the string and Sky Wolf the other. With the string slack, Winged Wolf sang the HU from the heart chakra, tightened it a little and HUed from the throat chakra, then holding it very tight, she sang from the crown chakra.

"A - A - A - A - A[1]," touching the throat chakra.

*Sky Wolf: "A - A - A - A."*

"Very good. Now, E - E - E - E," touching the crown chakra.

*Sky Wolf: "E - E - E - E - E."*

Together they worked on the HU, lifting the sound from 'A' to 'E' for about fifteen minutes.

"When working with sounds, the throat resonates with the sound. When trained vocalists sing 'A-A-A,' the 'A' joins together in the throat chakra. When they sing E-E-E-, the E joins together in the crown chakra."

"Let the HU fill your life. As you become one with the HU, you will begin to understand the Void. The HU will fill your life with understanding, with joy. You will know everything there is to know about the Void. To do this, you need to practice, practice, practice and practice!"

"When you touch Ichinen, (cat) she responds with a sound that resonates from her."

---

[1] On the lower scale, 'A' denotes the sound of the Throat chakra, whereas 'A' high resonates with the Third Eye. Likewise, 'E' low resonates with Third Eye Chakra, and 'E' high with the Crown Chakra.

*Sky Wolf: "How about Yoda and Sioux?"*

"Sioux makes a little, 'Enck, enck, enck' sometimes. But if Yoda, (Winged Wolf's small dog) has gone off someplace, she will howl."

"Try howling. Do you see how your whole body works to do it?"

# RESONANCE WITH THE HU

**Winged Wolf:** "May the blessings be.

"Let's talk about the HU. You are going to find the HU rearranging inside of you quite a bit in this next year. And, it will be rearranging inside of you is the resonance of the HU, the clarity, and the pitch. You are going to find it *presents* many changes as you are going through your practice.

"I would like you to start HUing one hour a day. There is a reason for this. Your life actually comes into harmony with the sound. The sound is an extension of the Void. It is the vibration that comes from the Void. It makes it a lot easier for you to carry out your day, and a lot easier for you to have a quiet mind. You will find that your opportunities in business and your dealings with other people will be smoother, because you will be taking the edge off yourself, before you get out into the world.

"Now, I know that seems like a long time. So what, you see? Some days, you are going to find, 'Well I can't do that, I'm in a hurry. I woke up late. Blah blah.' Well, you can HU in the car. This does not mean that you lose your concentration. The idea is to always be centered at the Third Eye when you are HUing, otherwise you are going to get spacy. If you have your attention on your job, or something that you are going to be doing while you are HUing, you are going to get spacy. Do not do that! You have to stay centered. *The whole idea is to stay centered as Soul, stay grounded as Soul.* It is just like you have a rope at the base of your spine, pulling you right into the earth, keeping you grounded.

"This is not a flaky path. It is not a path where you are off traveling everywhere in the astral body while you are here. You might be doing that, as well; (referring to an

191

advanced movement of consciousness) but, you will learn about that later but you will never be experiencing it in a flaky way. You will be integrated. It is very important that you stay here *now* in whatever you are doing, especially singing the HU.

"If you are driving the car, you are driving the car. Do you see? You are one with the wheel. If you are sounding the HU, the vibrations of your own body begin to blend with the HU.

"It is good for your health. It is an easy way to get the edges off your vibrations. Your health improves. Isn't it wonderful? You might find that you arrive at work with a little extra pink in your cheeks, and it is all natural. You save money on make up. (laughs). When you get to work, after the edges are taken off of your own vibrations, you will walk into a place, and you will be able to perceive the energy there. It will take a lot of question out of your life. You are putting yourself in harmony with the Void, in harmony with your own path, not someone else's path. You are centering yourself As Soul.

"But, there again, if you are off wandering in your imagination somewhere else, you are not being as Soul. Stay present. Learn to operate as Soul. Operating as Soul means you stay present.

"You do not have to pre-meditate all the details of what you are going to do in the workplace before you get there. 'Oh, how am I going to solve this problem and that problem.' You do not have to do that. As Soul, you can bypass all of that. As Soul, you can walk and harmonize with the situation; see what is going on and not get frazzled by it. You can deal with what is there. This is really important. Do not try to pre-meditate what is going to happen at a meeting or anything else. I don't want you to get in there and say, 'Oh, I was pleasantly surprised. I was expecting the worst. You know, Murphy's Law, expect the worst.' You set negative energy in motion, even though maybe it turned around. That is working with the law of reversed effort. It is not a healthy way to operate, and, about 80% of the time it will backfire on you. So, why do it that way? You have already done it that way a million times without happy results. Learn to operate As Soul!

"*Your empowerment exists in the present moment,* not outside of the present moment. Your empowerment does not exist in your yesterdays. It does not exist tomorrow. It exists right now, and you are unlimited by who you are, right now, if you are living the present moment. All the term 'Elder' means is that you have come to a point where you can live as Soul, because you have taken a good enough look at yourself. You have weeded through certain things and you are beginning to settle down and not operate out of your mind so much. You are where you are, because that's where you are! We do not have any 'pretend' positions here. Authenticity is the name of the game.

"If you get hung up in competition, or rushing, pushing for position, you won't get anywhere. You are stuck. That is what you call a stuck person. If you see your peers doing it, just love them. Have compassion for them. Do not get stuck yourself. Do not pass judgment. If you are passing judgment, you are going to get stuck! Perceive the energy that is there. Accept everybody for where they are, and accept yourself. You are not in a hurry to do anything. You walk at your pace. You are the one holding the drum mallet. You bang the drum. I might grab your hand once in a while and give it a few extra beats. Some of you, I cannot do that with; but when you become Elder, I should be able to do that. So, some of you who are sitting on the edge, pay attention. If you do not allow me to take hold of your mallet hand, and give it a few jerks once in awhile, you are going to find yourself running away. That's okay too.

"Don't worry, if I pick at you a little bit. It doesn't matter. If I'm picking at you a little bit, it just means that I want you to notice something and you are not paying attention. I know. I hear the stories behind my back, 'The Eagle pecks and the Wolf nips' or whatever. That's okay. That means you are paying attention, if you recognize it. That makes me happy.

"There are a few of you who call me up on the phone and you talk so fast that I can't get a word in edgewise and then you say, 'Thanks a lot.' You don't want a reply. Well, that is okay. I will let you get away with that for awhile, but, eventually I'll get through to you.

"Your journey (lesson) is like your home. That is how you live life, out of that journey. When you peek under the curtain, you are like a visitor to a strange land, so that when you at last journey on those different subjects, you will really soar with them.

"The name of our work together is 'empowerment'. I am doing everything I can to see to it that nothing holds you back, to get the door flung open so that, when you are ready to walk through it, to live in that spot for awhile, you are going to be prepared to see all kinds of things, that otherwise may take you longer to see.

"When I ask you to stay on a journey for longer than usual, you might say, 'Oh well, I understand that journey. I already know that one. I want to move on. I just want to get a report out.' Well, just sitting here, in the seat where you are sitting, for a few minutes, don't you see things that you didn't see when you first sat down? If you sat here all day, do you know how much you would see? There is so much to see that you can't see in a hurry. You can get a glimpse of it, and pick out little pieces, but, there is so much more to see. And, if you are so worried about hurrying, you are not living in the present moment. Stay here now, in the present moment! See everything you can from this present moment.

"Do not be satisfied with what you think you see. You know, move the gravel around. (Moves her foot on the gravel pavement). What is underneath there? What is it made of? Always pay attention like you are at the edge of discovery, at the edge of yourself - like you are wearing a capsule. Push your energy right to the edge of yourself, like you are wearing this capsule. Listen at the edge of your capsule. Push your energy right to the edge of it, looking out! Looking out! Don't sink inward, looking at yourself, watching yourself do the journeys, watching yourself not moving forward and moving forward. All it does when you get caught up staring at your feelings, is make you uncomfortable with where you are. You know, it makes you want to rush forward, or stare. 'Oh, I have come this far.' It is all right to take a look once in a while, but do not get hung up in that.

"The only place that is important, is here, now. Here, Now! **HERE, NOW!** Everything else unfolds. I will never try to hold you back. I want you to get there more than anybody else. And, you are already doing it, but, there is going to be so much more.

"Don't scrutinize each other. Have compassion. Each one of you has an individual relationship with me, based on the way you want it, not the way I want it. By that I mean you are yourself and I treat you as an individual. If I ignore you, I ignore you for a reason. If I give you lots of attention, I give you lots of attention for a reason, and not always because you are so wonderful. See, you decide what our relationship is by being yourself. If you want our relationship to be something else, then you adjust yourself, but do not try to be like somebody else. If you adjust yourself, you adjust parts of yourself that bring out different responses in me. I am your mirror.

"Do not be competitive and copy someone else because nobody is better than anybody else and that includes myself. I am Soul just like you are Soul. And it is not your Soul, or my Soul. We are *One*.

"Fantasy, and I will probably speak about this again, watch your fantasies. Fantasy is not the way. I know you were taught that imagination will give you everything. Visualize this. Fantasize that. Well, you know what? You visualize and fantasize all you like and what do you end up with? A fantasy. You might have fun fooling a few people and having them play along with it, but you are still just having a fantasy. Be Here Now!

"This is not fantasy. This is real empowerment. Allow it to occur. You do not need fantasy. You need fantasy when you don't know how to get where you are going. You are frustrated which is really anger. So, you are in the paper bag, and the only way you can stand to be caught in this paper bag, because you don't know how to kick out of it, not realizing it's only paper, is you create these fantasies. We'll talk about fantasy again. I just wanted to throw it out there. *

"*Your empowerment exits in the present moment, not outside of the present moment. It does not exist tomorrow. It exists right now, and you are unlimited by who you are, right now, if you are living the present moment.*"

"There is so much power in a moment of life, in the capsule of this moment, you do not need fantasy. In real reality, there is so much power. There is so much excitement. There is no boredom. Stop pushing your aura and spilling your energy in front of you, throwing love out to the world. Stop doing that kind of thing. That is a fantasy to think that you are helping someone. You are getting into their private psychic space. You are manipulating them. The Shaman Consciousness does not manipulate. *The Shaman Consciousness does not manipulate.* You will probably hear me say that seven hundred and forty two million times before we are done. Get it into your head. I do not mean that the Shaman Consciousness does not manipulate in certain situations. I mean,

# IT DOES NOT MANIPULATE! EVER!

"You do not have to manipulate your day, or people who make up your day. If you do, you will get into, 'Well, if I don't treat my wife a certain way, she will handle me!' That's not true. You be as Soul. Center yourself. Let each person have their own experience and share what you can and you will find that you will enjoy life much more. Don't blame problems on your spouse and your family. There is nothing wrong with your spouse or your family. You live As Soul."

# SHANUNPA

**Winged Wolf:** "One of the most important practices in the attainment of Shaman Consciousness is the art of Shanunpa, which is the art of imitation. When you want to understand the nature of any living person or thing, you imitate it to acquire this understanding."

(Speaking to Sky Wolf, she continued),

"A few moments ago, I heard the sound of tremendous effort in flight and looked up. Two crows were flying through the thick, moist air on this rainy day. The sound of that movement was great, which is why I made you imitate the sound even though you could not hear it. That way, you would know what the crows were feeling while flying through the air. On a heavy moisture day, one rarely sees birds in flight, because of the effort it takes. When you and I imitated the birds together, you could feel how much of your body had to move to make enough motion to push the air out, so you knew what it was like to be a crow in flight.

"This is a very important lesson. When you see things moving in nature, for instance, when you see a deer running, take a moment out of your daily life and imitate the movement of that deer. Experience what it feels like. Imitate the movement with your body. You will come to know 'stalking' by imitating.

"Stalking is imitation of movement to become one with that which is being stalked. You become in tune with another person, animal, or thing. If you want to know what I am about, stalk me, imitate me! Walk like me in the spirit of learning, for the purpose of knowing what I am about. I don't care if you imitate my speech, if it is done in

Shanunpa. I would be grateful for you to do so! So, imitate me!

"Now, we are not talking about making fun of somebody on the street and having a laugh at someone's expense. Only a little-minded person behaves that way. We are speaking about Shanunpa, which is learning the energy of another person, animal or thing through the art of imitation."

*"Shanunpa is the art of imitation. When you want to understand the nature of any living person or thing, you imitate it to acquire this understanding."*

# PRESENTING THE "VOID"

**Winged Wolf:** "When HU ᴜᴜᴜᴜᴜᴜᴜᴜᴜᴜᴜᴜᴜᴜᴜᴜᴜᴜᴜᴜ is sounded in the Universe, it is the Void expressing Itself. When the sound of the pitch is changed, raised or lowered, this is the way the Void presents. Just as a carpenter takes his hammer and nails and does his work, this is the Void presenting. As the hammer is raised, it will have a steady sound and as the hammer hits the nail, it will make a different sound.

"The clarity of this *presenting* is very important for every person to know. When this clarity is known, you will understand the Void.

"When a crow flies over, its wings make a sound in the air. It sounds like swosh, swosh, swosh. This is the same thing, the Void is presenting. As Sioux is walking around outside the Happy House among the leaves, her feet are sounding the Void - crunch, crunch, crunch. The sound of the Void goes on like this forever."

*Sky Wolf: "Does it go on twenty four hours a day?"*

"Yes, twenty four hours a day. When you are sleeping the sound will be a level 'zzzzzzzzzzzzzzzz'. When you get up and start moving around, it will raise and lower in pitch."

*Sky Wolf: "What about an ant?"*

"An ant would make a soft, soft cracking sound but it would be clearly a sound from the Void. A bee makes a buzz, buzz, buzz sound as it flies around."

# DREAMING

**Winged Wolf:** "Today's talk is about dreaming. Was there a particular facet of dreaming we wanted to discuss, or just dreaming?"

*Two Eagles: "Going back to the same place in the dream."*

"Dreaming. We sit here looking at each other dreaming. Yesterday morning we were sitting and looking at each other dreaming. Today we are doing it as well, same place, same time.

"Dreaming. It wasn't very complicated to get here was it? We simply came here to this meeting place at the agreed time, looked at each other and that was the dream. All life is dreaming. *All* life is dreaming.

"If there was not the dream, there would be no life. There is no separation in saying I am asleep dreaming and I am awake in this life dreaming; except that, when the body is asleep dreaming, the mind all of a sudden is filled with a lot of messages stored up from during the awake dreaming time that did not come through clearly. So, at night, when you go to sleep, what happens? All the messages that were stored up in your brain come rushing forth to express themselves. Because they come rushing forth to express themselves, they come out in an odd fashion, not in sequence. They also come out in a symbolic way. They will come out with you doing bazaar things, because all the circuitry in the brain is coming together. The wires are clicking, interacting, and short circuiting, so, it comes out as symbolic messages.

"Sometimes, you can go to sleep at night and symbolic dreaming does not occur, because there is no short circuitry. Instead, what you get is perfect clarity and, in the dream, you cannot really tell if your body is asleep or awake. This means that during the day you were living clearly as Soul, so there were not stored-up messages.

"Messages are stored during the day when there are points of confusion. When a person is not living as Soul, they are in conflict much of the time with, 'Well, is it this way? Or, is it that way?' Do you see? If there is no conflict when you go to sleep at night, there is no short circuitry of the brain. If you were living as Soul during the day, there would be no short circuitry of the brain and so you would not dream at all. When you do have dreams, which can be defined as igniting moments of life into images or a succession of images passing through the mind, it is Soul igniting those images into the brain, using the brain.

"Soul produces images in the brain for a specific intent such as, I will meet you in a classroom sometime, or sometimes we will go for a hike up on a hill, or you will have a very clear dream with someone where you are having an actual meeting, an occurrence with that person. Sometimes that person is deceased, sometimes not. Now, that is when Soul is in command of the brain. Quite a difference there!

"When a person is living in conflict, the brain is in control during the day, and, as a result, there is constant conflict, constant duality. There is this side versus that side. There is always the dilemma, this way versus that way. When this occurs during the day, it affects your sleep at night. When you go to sleep you see dual images and short circuitry occurs in your brain. So, people spend lifetimes, you know, searching books, trying to figure out the symbology of these experiences. I say to you, *it doesn't matter.*

"If you are living as Soul, you will not be having symbolic type dreams. If you learn to live as Soul centered at the Third Eye, something begins to happen, a settling down, a stability, a grounding so that each image that comes into the brain is directed by Soul. The brain is enlivened to show an image of that direction.

"It takes awhile to attain self mastery. You are in charge of your life. What you look at, you look at consciously, and that then becomes a dream image. A dream image again, is being nothing more than an image striking a center in the brain and producing a picture. The picture, because we have human eyes, is then projected outward into the environment. It is like a three dimensional movie. You begin to live in it. This is what we do as human beings. We project dream images to have a life to live in an environment.

"Without dream images, there would be no environment. There is nothing but the Void, this moment in the Void. There is nothing else. You produce dream images as Soul and make a three dimensional environment for yourselves to walk around in."

*Wings of Change: "While your brain sleeps at night, what happens to your consciousness?"*

"It sleeps. It is a time when you are not producing images. There is nothing but stillness. The Void is all stillness. Mental activity produces motion which produces consciousness of that motion. This produces more movement, more consciousness, more awareness. This is the whole cycle of life, which is rather a large chunk. This is something that will have to be reviewed many, many times and each time you review it, you will get it differently. So you see, the complexity of life that everybody is always trying to solve, does not exist, except in the complexity of the individual dreamer. That is why there are a million books describing, at great length, so many aspects of the human being, of the environment, of the animal kingdom, of the insect kingdom, of Mother

Earth, of Father Sky, of the Universe, because *all* of these things only exist in the dreamer.

"As you walk out into the environment and you look at something, an image strikes in your brain and that enlarges. Where your attention is, is what enlarges."

*Two Eagles: "So that is what happened when Wolfsong saw a face in the tree? She placed her attention there?"*

"She placed her attention on the tree, then she saw the face, and then the face enlarged itself. The face was an image that she was carrying inside of her own mind at the time she looked at the tree, but when she saw it in the tree, it began to enlarge. This three dimensional life is of your own invention."

*Wings of Change: "Does that mean that we dreamed the animals, trees, and all the other consciousness, or are they dreaming themselves?"*

"They are dreaming themselves. That is why they can be so demanding and so imposing. Their interaction with you, you dreamed. Their place in your life just, as your place in their life, they dreamed."

*Standing Turtle: "What about the wind that has been buzzing around here the past fifteen minutes?"*

"Why wouldn't it?"

*Standing Turtle: "Well, it is unusual. We have never had wind like that before. The plastic covering on the windows of the Happy House has been frantically expanding and collapsing from the wind."*

"We are reaching outside of the ordinary images of life and, when you do that, it stirs the environment. Oh! Bong! Bing! Pow! Pah! (Laughs)

204

*Wings of Change: "And the purpose for us as Soul is to have experience."*

"To become aware of who you are; to become aware of the Void Self; the God Self within you; to become aware that you, the dreamer are IT. And, you become aware of that through your awareness and then through the experience of practicing that awareness. Remember, this is the Shamanic path, the path of experience, which is what the Shaman Path means."

*"People spend lifetimes searching books trying to figure out the symbology of their dreams. I say to you, it doesn't matter. If you had been living as Soul, you would not be having symbolic dreams."*

# REMAKING THE DREAM

Winged Wolf closed the HUing session, "May the blessings be," and nodded her acknowledgment to Sky Wolf for his HUing.

*Sky Wolf: "It is different."*

**Winged Wolf:** "It will become more and more different as time goes on. One of the things that is happening to you is that you are becoming tuned in to the idea of vibration, in a way that you have never been before.

"A few weeks ago, you said that you had a dream about the sound of the vibration, and you said, you felt you were hearing vibrations in your dream. This is how life begins, in a dream. You see, before the dream of life began, there was nothing. Nothing at all. Nothing existed. Likewise, before your dream, you had no sensation of sound, and then, as you begin to fill up a dream you are dreaming, it begins to materialize.

"You are now exhibiting the HU. A great vibration fills your body and consumes your mind. This vibration begins to mobilize certain centers in the brain that have been dormant as you are becoming more attuned to the vibration. When you deliberately produce a vibration, it becomes alive in you. You carry it inside of you as you go about your day and into your sleep at night, where there is less paradoxical or conflicting aliveness in your mind. In other words, you begin to easily feel the vibration in your sleep, and what happens? Suddenly, you take on a new aliveness. Please pay attention. We are getting to the crux of it all. All life is a feeling. Without awareness, which results as FEELING, part of your life does not exist. For you, Sky Wolf, hearing does not exist, but it is beginning to. Hearing is beginning to exist.

"The person who does not have sight, may develop sight by singing the HU every day, day in and day out! And, this person who is learning to be centered at the Third Eye, the seat of Soul, will begin to have visions when asleep. The visions, then, produce light and images. And maybe an aliveness comes into that individual's brain to see.

"It is the same thing with one who is deaf, and also to a person with limitations in another way. Everybody has some kind of limitation they have set upon themselves.

"Some people have a disease in their body, and they have set a limitation for themselves in that way. Other people have set limitations on themselves through hardened attitudes and opinions.

"When this occurs, part of them becomes encased in stone. Now, they must break that part out of the stone (Speaking to Sky Wolf). "You were born not hearing, therefore, you imposed the limitation of no sound in a previous life. Perhaps you had suffered intense fear, so intense that the fear consumed you, and you shut down your hearing to escape it. Maybe it was the sound of a bomb exploding, coupled with the horrifying sounds of injured people screaming, which caused your hearing loss."

(Speaking to Standing Turtle)
"People who have the nature to want to look at something and pick it apart to analyze it in order to discern it, are setting a limitation on themselves. It is just as much of a limitation as one who cannot hear.

"Everybody has something. Everybody has something!

"I have another Sage apprentice whose life is death when she is not in the limelight. You know!" (laughing), "And, that is just another hang-up. It was formed by learned attitudes and opinions when the person was a child. These myths are prisons. Do you see? People create

207

prisons for themselves. I have another apprentice who feels she can only succeed through suffering. You see, through feeling pain, she believed she was getting somewhere. She was working hard and suffering, and she was getting nowhere! Now, she has learned that she does not have to suffer, that her pain was a prison.

"When you try to correct something, the longer you have had it, the harder it is to correct. If you go to a doctor about a pain in your back, and say, 'I have had pain in my back for one week,' the doctor knows he can cure it very quickly. But, if you have had pain in your back for twenty years, it is a chronic problem and it is more difficult to heal. So, it only stands to reason that, if you have carried something forward from a previous life, it is not quite as simple as taking care of something that has just developed within the week. This is why we no longer sweep anything under the rug.

"Rather than sweeping anything under the rug in our daily lives, we reclaim the energy from it, as you are taught in your apprentice journeys.

"There is no reason you cannot resolve the karma from your past lives. The solution is to live wholeheartedly this moment, rather than focusing on karma from the past. Give yourself to the HU! Give yourself to living in the center of the Third Eye.

"You, Standing Turtle, say, 'Well, I don't know if I can change. Such and so is from the very core of my being.' It's not so. The condition can change! When I say change, I mean you can be freed from it. It can still be sitting around in your periphery, but you don't have to pick it up and use it.

(Speaking to Sky Wolf)

"Your prison, being deaf, is a different kind of prison. You need to enrich yourself so fully in the present moment that whatever occurs, will occur, and that occurrence will be an aliveness of who you are. Bits and pieces of your prison will gradually fall away as you go. Pay no attention to them whatsoever. Stay totally focused on the present moment. *Totally* give yourself to the present moment.

"Liberation begins in the dream, the dream from one who is deaf, who feels the vibration, and then hears the sound of the vibration. This is why I show you motion in life, and want you to imitate it. If you observe the movement of a branch, then I want you to imitate the movement of the branch. That way you can begin to feel the vibration and let that sound come alive in you, too. Do you see how it begins? It begins in the dream. All life is a dream. You made the dream, but you can re-make the dream at anytime."

# THE LOVER AND THE BELOVED

**Winged Wolf:** "A long time ago the atom split. There was a positive electron and a negative electron, two halves to a whole. Human Beings presently replicate that condition as do animals and insects. Usually, the energies live apart. While there are some androgynous insects, and worms are certainly androgynous, animals do not presently have the capacity of merging those two halves again. Humans do, endowed with an awareness of their consciousness.

"We are speaking of the human being becoming a holistic entity. When a human being becomes holistic unto theirself, that division of masculine and feminine still exists, but it exists differently. A man can develop traits that are female in that he becomes integrated with female traits, and likewise, a female can develop traits that are male; that is, she becomes integrated, as well. The part that integrates is the part of balance contained in each gender.

"Energies merge when you *look* beyond dualities and begin to see life as a whole, and when you appreciate its wholeness. Now, the key words I just used were *appreciate its wholeness*.

"When a couple genuinely falls in love, the union of love-making becomes a merging of energies that is no longer sex. In contrast, when a man and a woman come together out of physical attraction alone, and quickly 'hop into the sack', they are responding to an animal instinct, out of which they evolved before becoming human.

"A merging of masculine and feminine energies takes place when there is balance within the individuals involved, when both individuals are ready to stand tall and strong together, looking in the same direction, not one leaning upon the other. A friendship exists between them that uplifts them into the integrated consciousness.

"That merger of masculine and feminine energies within an individual does not usually take place in a coupling experience. It is very nice for those involved in that type of experience and it can be a deeply honorable experience, but the real merger of energies comes to an individual who lives as Soul. If they find someone with whom they can share experiences with, who is on the same level, that is wonderful, but rare. Two people who live as Soul, can have intimate experiences together that are quite special. Their experiences have moved out of the sexual realm and into the divine love realm.

"An individual who chooses not to have a partner in life, or who has not found that partner in life as yet, can experience being whole as Soul.

"Because you do not have a mate in life does not mean that you cannot experience complete joy. One experience is not better than the other. They are simply different experiences.

"A heightened part of the merger between masculine and feminine energies is forward movement on the Path. When you live as Soul, you love life whole-heartedly. Every waking moment is a joy. Friends in life are very dear to you, but you make no demands of them. You are both the masculine side and the feminine side of all relationships. Even in a man-woman relationship as Soul, you are both. As both, you never use intimacy to manipulate the other person, to try to get something you want, because that deception immediately splits the atom again.

"This cliché: 'I am a woman finagling a man', or 'I am a man finagling a woman', is manipulation. To have a relationship on such a casual basis is an inferior experience in every way. You might enjoy an intoxicating night, but the experience cannot enhance your life. It pulls you down to animal consciousness.

"Our society is suffering from AIDS, which is a plague. Of course, there are some unusual circumstances that can infect one with AIDS, but the main cause is promiscuous sex. That means using sex like it was a cookie.

"I hear people talking about making love all the time, and so do you. That is not making love. They are going out for one-night stands, or living with someone because they do not want to live alone. They want someone to share the rent and sexual experience, but they do not really feel close to the person with whom they are sharing. Or, maybe the relationship is a lopsided type of experience, where one person is in love with the other, but the other person does not feel love for them; so, there is abuse involved. That kind of love is insanity!

"When people fall in love and their life is out of control, they are insane. That is what insanity is - *It is being out of control of your life!* Your life becomes chaotic. All kinds of problems arise, and if you have been really careless, it ends up in disease, such as AIDS.

"You know, we like to blame AIDS on every other reason in the world, because we do not want to take a look at the behavior of our society. We do not want to admit what the cause is, to the point where it is almost covered over now. No longer do people look at it for what it is. It is so prevalent, it has become merged into society itself. Both heterosexual and homosexual relationships are in danger, and children are now being born with it. There are now all sorts of ways to transmit AIDS. People have lost recognition of the disease's original cause, promiscuous sex.

"Anyway, I do not want to harp on that. I simply want to make you aware of your activities in life so that you can begin to take stock of yourself as you are going toward being a Spiritual Warrior.

"This talk, 'the Lover and the Beloved', the merger of the masculine and feminine energies, has a greater side to it. The greater side, of becoming whole unto yourself, results from *an upliftment in consciousness.* It is your awareness reaching out to touch life. You observe the traits of one sex versus another sex, and those positive traits become merged into the whole. A woman learns perseverance. A man learns joy. The sharing experience of life in each individual becomes paramount.

"When an individual learns to live as Soul, which is defined as living with a quiet mind, the halves are integrated, because there is no conflict to separate them. One who lives in Buddha Consciousness, or Christ Consciousness, or Shaman Consciousness is integrated and whole. The mind is quiet. However, there is one discomfort to having a quiet mind: The noise of other people's minds can get very intense sometimes.

"When we close here, you are going to enter into silence, which will be a very exciting experience for you, because at first you are going to feel you have to talk to everyone. It always happens. You suddenly think of a million things you have to say. But just this one night, I want you to have this experience of verbally shutting down. At first your thoughts may be active but, remember, you do have the capability of going into Soul Vision. Every time you feel that you have to say something, use that urge as a trigger into Soul Vision, focused at the Third Eye. Find that quiet place inside of yourself. It is a very subtle discovery.

"I am going to help you. I am going to work with you, not verbally, but very quietly. When you enter into the silence, I may be looking at you and you may be looking at me, or you may have a black screen filled with light, which is all a black screen is, intense light turned into darkness. *Look* out of yourself.

"Those of you who went walking with me today, practiced looking out of yourselves, not inwardly to see your feelings about things, but looking out to experience the beautiful lake. We witnessed the aliveness, the movement of the water, and the wind blowing across it. And, you imitated the sounds you heard, which gave you a deeper understanding of what the lake was all about. The light was beautiful. The shadows were beautiful. It was a picture that was clearly perceived, and you got the idea of perceiving, of looking without mental comment.

"I am the lover and you are the beloved. I love each one of you and it is for this reason that I give you the gift of silence.

"Notice that in quiet, there is still noise. It goes both ways. And, while you are listening, listen to hear if maybe there is a sweet silent sound coming to you. The vibration of the HU may be resonating inside of you. Look out of yourself so that you feel your energy about a foot in front of your face.

"Be still. Be quiet. While you are verbally quiet, you may find that quiet space inside of yourself. You may have a burst of sudden joy fill up around your heart area. Bliss. It may feel as though you can feel your heart singing. This experience can only occur when you can look out of yourself, without mental comment.

"Looking out means you look out of yourself as Soul. You observe. You can laugh and have fun, but, for the next few hours pull your energy in.

"When you become adept at being quiet, the merger with the Consciousness, with the Shaman Consciousness, will be yours, and the crown will be on your head, as well.

"Are there any questions, comments, or discussion? Please do not hold back. *Talk to me.*"

*Eagle Tribe Member: "What about energy?"*

"You transmute energy by letting it go, by taking your attention off it and getting into Soul Vision. If you worry about energy, then you are holding it up here saying, 'Oh! I don't know what to do about it'. By doing this, it exists. If you let it go, it no longer exists. Energy does dissipate. However, when you worry, you are intensifying that which you do not want to send out.

"The world is filled with thought forms. Actually, the world was/is created by thought forms. It is not healthy for the environment for you to project emotional images into it, and it's not healthy for you to do it. Whatever you put out there, comes back to you in some way, maybe not that day, but in some other experience. It always goes full circle. What goes around, comes around; but to sit and worry about what you did, intensifies your fear not only for yourself but for the environment at large.

"*Do not feel guilty, guilt is an illusion*. Feeling guilty is an emotion which springs from behavior learned in the past from people making you feel guilty and fearful.

"We had an experience here earlier. People were telling me about their relationship with a religious organization. One of the things that was so terrifying to them was that this religious path printed a statement similar to this: 'If you move away from the path you will not find God for eons of time.' I do not recall the exact verbiage. Even though the follower may say that s/he does not believe it, the threat is stuck in their mind that s/he are going to be punished forever. Any teaching that uses fear to hold you, is a limited teaching. Put the fear in your life aside. Put the guilt in your life aside and live wholeheartedly as Soul.

"Stop the worry. All worry gets you is more worry. If you worry about something, it grows. Fear can become a huge, tremendous monster. Once one begins to worry about something, the worry builds new worries. Let it go!"

*Grounded in Soul: "Can hypnotherapy be done on the path of Soul?"*

"That is a very important question. Wings of Change (she is a mental health professional), do you want to come over here and speak?"

*Wings of Change: "So the question was, can hypnotherapy be done on the Path of Soul? The difference is that hypnotherapy neutralizes or distracts the conscious mind and works with the subconscious, whereas the Path of Soul quiets the conscious mind. When a person experiences hypnotherapy to correct a problem, the problem may in fact be corrected. Patients may quit smoking, or eat less, but that has not altered the conscious mind, so, the person really has learned nothing about managing h/his life."*

"You see, the Path of Soul wakes a person up. Hypnotherapy makes numb certain areas in the brain so that other areas can open up. So, you have put one area to sleep in order to wake up another area. What do you have? Do you see? The *whole* person has to be awake, to live as Soul.

"I heard a story from one of my apprentices who went to a hypnotherapist to quit smoking, but she picked up another habit to replace it. So, what good is that?"

*Grounded in Soul: "What are your thoughts on past life regression work?"*

"What value does past life regression have? You may have heard people claim they have had success with it, but how does that benefit the individual? It truly does not.

"You see, today you are everyone you have ever been. If you want to know who you have been, just look at your life now. You are a composite of your experiences from all your lives, past and present. When you learn to

216

live as Soul, and learn to know yourself as Soul, those bits and pieces, those imprints that you carry with you, will become very clear. Living as Soul is an adventure, because it really tells you everything you want to know, and you get your answers yourself. Somebody else is not meddling around in your mind.

"The mind is a record keeper. There are many things lodged in one's mind. A good therapist can help somebody see those things and get them to turn lodged things loose, by not by staring at them.

"Part of the difficulty with therapy is that many times a therapist will keep a person in therapy long past the time necessary to benefit them. They allow their subjects to become self-indulgent, to stare inwardly at themselves and feel sorry for themselves, looking at the same things over and over and over again, questioning the same thing over again and digging up more dirt from the past. Well, you know, it is a big trash can, isn't it? As long as you are in there, smelling all that old rotten garbage, how are you going to know what life is about? So, a good therapist, to me, is one who gets a person to look at their difficulty and then gets them out of the office. You know, move them on!

"Take a look at the present moment of your life. How can you improve it? If something shows up in the history book of your past that has to be noticed, then take a look at it, and get rid of it. Don't hang on to it. Don't keep scratching the scab off the wound, watching the blood ooze out.

"Is there anybody else?"

*Eagle Tribe Member: "Can you explain a little about chanting or HUing?"*

"The pitch is not the key to chanting, clarity is. It has nothing to do with the depth of your voice. You might have to chant at a lower pitch for awhile to get the clarity. It's the clarity that is most important. HU with whatever pitch feels comfortable to you, and then raise it. Play with it, bringing it up and then down, but stay at a comfortable pitch. That is the important part."

*Eagle Tribe Member: "Would you please explain what you mean by 'clarity in a person's HU?"*

"Let us HU! I want you to listen to the clarity, otherwise, we will just get caught up in mental gymnastics. If this does not help, we will talk again. Is that fair enough?
"We take a few deep breaths in the beginning to relax and to energize our bodies. Continue breathing deeply as you are HUing."

Winged Wolf takes three deep breaths and begins the HU Song.

## "HUUUUUUUUUUUUUUUUUUUUUUUUUUUUUUUU

A huge shooting star or orange-yellow comet raced across the sky.

# THE STAINLESS SKY

**Winged Wolf:** "This talk can only be made because you are ready to hear it. Like all the discussions we have had together, I can only speak when you are ready.

"The stainless sky is the condition of a Thunder-being. The stainless sky has ingredients to it which makes it stainless. A stainless sky is a clear blue sky with no clouds. It has no markings of any kind. It is a stainless sky.

"The first very great ingredient of a stainless sky is the teachings. All along, I always give you the teachings as quickly as you can receive them. Never do I hold back. Never could I hold back, because as soon as you are ready to receive, it comes from me, through me. I am a vehicle for the Void. I am not allowed to discriminate and say, 'You get this and you do not get that'. I do not have any mental contraptions going on saying, 'This is and this is not'. Simply, when you are ready to receive, I am ready to speak.

"So the teachings you have been getting are because you are ready to receive them. If you are not ready to receive them, you would not have received them. Because you have been ready to receive them, those who are approaching the pathway can also hear them to the degree that they can hear them. The teachings are the first ingredient. I cannot get them out fast enough, as you know, but we are getting them out. It is important for you to know about these teachings.

"It is important for you to understand responsibility and creation and all sorts of things, but another part of the teachings is your journey. Your journey is the house in which you live. Each journey takes you deeper and deeper into a level of consciousness where you can receive the teachings more fully.

219

"The book that we are doing about these teachings, *'Dialogues with a Shaman Teacher'* can be read on many levels. It can be read by a beginner and it can be read by a Thunderbeing. It can be read by anyone. The teachings will be received according to the houses in which people live, whether they be apprentices or not.

"It is important then for you to have your journeys. Your journeys are not just words on a paper. If they were, we could put them in any book or accompany them in this book. But, your journeys are experiential, and they enliven a part of you as Soul that was not awake before. Each journey is a capsule and it explodes a whole new world inside of you. To say you do not need certain journeys is a fallacy. Each journey is so vitally important. All the teachings in this book are meant to accompany those journeys and fill in the spaces. So, the teachings are the first ingredient of the stainless sky.

"The second is clarity. Each of you has astounding clarity from where you stand and I honor you for it. I listened to you speak at 'The Gathering'. You were clear and giving, only what you did not know, was not clear. Some of those spaces are filled in now and that part of you is clear. Clarity is truly being able to live the teachings, to understand them in their fullest, not just in an intellectual way, but to be able to perceive the energy of the teachings so that the clarity can roll from your lips or from your life. This is a vital ingredient of the stainless sky. There is no way around it.

"The third vitally important ingredient of the stainless sky is balance. Without balance, you cannot live the teachings. You will fall and bring others with you. *Balance* has to be sustained, balance that is tested, not balance today and imbalance tomorrow. It is when you go out into the world and can maintain that balance in the toughest situations with your families. Can you be with your families and be in balance? Can you be with your

220

job and be in balance? Can you be in life doing anything and maintain that balance? The balance is the journey home where you are to live. You see, there is much to work on with each journey. It is your job to make each step of your journey a moment of balance, to take it, live it, and perfect it. Perfect it in such a way that your life becomes what you want it to be.

"You early journeyers, initiates, apprentices who are paving the way on this path with this teacher have a tough job. Nobody opened the gates for you, do you see? The path has been a lot of, 'Oh, what do I do now?' waiting for the next journey.

"I did not come with a manual. I am writing that manual. It was never put down before and I do not know of any teaching anywhere that has ever put it down in such exacting steps, so there is nothing from which to copy. There are no patterns. All I have is my own experience as an apprentice. Do you see? I am not withholding anything from you. I am giving it to you as quickly as I can and you are getting very close, each of you, in your own way, very close to the stainless sky.

"So there is no need to ever compare yourselves, one to the other. All that does is to put a cloud in the sky. The sky has to be clear. It cannot be filled with comparisons or self doubt. Self doubt puts a cloud in the sky. Any hole in any journey that has not been completed puts a cloud in the sky. You know where your holes are. I know where they are too. If I could put a piece of scotch tape over them and say, 'Let's go anyway', I would, but that scotch tape shows up in a stainless sky. It is a mark up there in that clear blue.

"You are not far away. Look what you have gotten from the teachings in just a few days. Do you see? Do not be impatient. You can only swallow water as fast as you can get it down your throat. I can only tell you things as you are ready, otherwise I cannot speak because you would not hear what I have to say. Someday again, this same subject will be taken up but it will not be in the presence of people who are close to Thunderbeing, but in the presence of people who are Thunderbeing. It will have a whole different level to it again. Otherwise, when you become Thunderbeing, you are going to be chaffing at the bit to become Shaman and that would be wrong, because you cannot be Thunderbeing and be chaffing at the bit for anything.

"As Thunderbeing, you have a stainless sky. You want for nothing. Shaman Consciousness does not come because you are chasing it. It comes because it has to come into a stainless sky, and I am going to tell you the big secret ingredient of maintaining a stainless sky in moments when you do have it. I am not going to just give you a few ingredients and leave you. I am going to tell you the secret of it, so pay very close attention.

"You have to have a sustained stainless sky in the role of Thunderbeing for the Shaman Consciousness to come to you; for the power that you will wear. If you did not have the balance, you would wreak havoc in the world. And, I want to tell a little bit more about the havoc that you can wreak, before I tell you the secret of the stainless sky.

"As a Thunderbeing, you will have the power of attention, the power of divine love, and the power of compassion. These powers produce effects in the world that can be misused. Everything has its opposite. A Thunderbeing knows how to work with opposites. You will have to accept responsibility, sustained responsibility, in your personal environment, living in harmony, before you will be able to live with a sustained stainless sky, and before you will wear that power. That means you may not engage in anger for any reason. It is forbidden. Go out and stick your face into the mud. Do anything. Laugh at yourself. Do what is easiest for you to deflect it, not subdue it, or hold it in, which would amplify it. This is not a mental thing. *Get rid of it.* Transmute it in a way where no harm comes to you and the environment, or anyone in it.

"We will know, you and I, when that time comes. It can come in a moment. It has no time on it, but it is sustained. It must be tested, otherwise you will have the power to kill. There can be no stuck memories in you that contain anger. If you have sore spots, use the techniques that you have been given to release them. Anger is forbidden. If you flash anger, immediately break into laughter. Call yourself a fool. Make light of it in anyway that you can. If you fall into guilt, your anger will increase. Your anger will come up again, because you are set to test yourself. Rest assured, it will come. Be prepared. Set a trigger for Soul Vision.

"For God's sake, for the sake of the stainless sky that you are looking for individually, have compassion. Do not say, 'I told you so'. Do not needle somebody into anger. You will curse yourself into a position where you will be plagued by anger yourself.

"You cannot play the games of the 'little self' anymore. You are too far along on the path. I am sorry, it is over. No more picky little games, it is too dangerous. *Directness is your path.* Kindness is the way you carry it out. And, when you make a mistake, and you will, forgive yourself and quickly move out of it. If you stay in a state of anger for three seconds, you are in trouble. Drop it on the first second and allow the second second to settle it down.

"Carry some smelling salts or something strong in your pocket. When it rises up, take a sniff to shock you back to the present moment. Do not ask somebody else for help. You have to do it yourself. You are at a place now where you do not ask your spouse or a friend to help you in that way. You do it! You can talk to me about it

223

and you should talk to me about it, but you still end up doing it yourself.

Now, I promised you the secret of the stainless sky. I spoke to you before about the ancient art of *'looking'*, only briefly. It really contains the secret of perfection, perfection as the stainless sky. It has nothing to do with physical sight or physical hearing and yet it does, but not necessarily so. A blind person can practice the art of *'looking'*. A deaf person can practice the art of 'listening'.

"Being on the edge of your seat, or on the edge of yourself all the time, as if you were listening for something, is very important. To a deaf person that would be the same thing as sensing something very important about to happen and not trying to figure out what it is, but waiting on the edge. You have allowed yourself up to this moment, to be what you call comfortable, and it really is not. It is a pleasure thing where you just kind of kick back and lose the edge for living. Now I am asking you to refine that edge. It is very sharp. It is very thin. Listen. Listen. Sense it, not just with your ears. If you had no ears, if you did not hear, you could still sense it.

"Get your body in a sense of, I hate to use the word, 'expectation', there must be a better one. We have been through so much on that word."

*Wings of Change: "Anticipation?"*

"Anticipation, thank you. You can feel that something is out there, but not quite. There is no mental activity about it at all. The stainless sky is a perfectly blue clear sky that is in a state of waiting. It is in a state of listening, of sensing. There is not a wisp of air moving. You walk through life on a busy street, you could do this in downtown Detroit."

"Sit on the edge of your seat. Just always sit on the edge of your seat, relaxed but alert. This way, you are aware and alert to what is going on. This is the time of year that the tree frogs come alive. The rains are here. Listen to them intently. Sense them. Look at them. You can look at them with your senses and there is no conversation about it. There is no mental conversation going on whatsoever. This means, as you hear a croak, a flash or an image might appear. It is only an image, it has no words connected to it.

"Wherever you are, whatever you are doing, even if you are absorbed writing something, do it in that way. Can you feel your energy pushing against your skin? That is how you are to live. That does not mean your energy is not contained. You do not spread yourself everywhere, but your energy is up tight against your skin. Your skin is your capsule. Your skin is what keeps you contained, do you see? You can feel your energy against your skin. That is sitting on the edge of your seat! Isn't that exciting?

"So as you move towards the stainless sky in each moment, you are living with that energy, pushing against your skin. You are becoming more and more *that*.

"Relax. There is no such thing as distance. By now you should know that distance is an illusion. Live impeccably. Live wholeheartedly. Do not measure your deeds, just live them. That is the stainless sky. It is a state of being. *Heaven is only three inches above your head!*

"Number one, the teachings. Get the teachings. Then with clarity and balance, you have the power of the stainless sky. Then we can run into the cliff wall together!"

# BEYOND THE RAINBOW

**Winged Wolf:** "May the blessings be.

"So today you have some questions about enlightenment."

*Gazelle: "How does the New Age movement tie in with what we are doing?"*

"The New Age movement is a movement with a purpose and an energy-drive to bring about ways and means of finding enlightenment. Out of that, comes whatever path anybody can conjure up to follow. The New Age movement is a seeker's world. Unfortunately, many people have gotten caught up in seeking and have forgotten that they have to actually walk a path, meaning to experience life in order to understand what the path is about.

"New Agers are 'tryers', dabblers. They try a little of this and a little of that; dabble here and there which often-times leads achieving very little because they approach knowledge as though they are on pogo sticks. When you have decided upon a path, you want to walk it as far as it will take you, so that you can see what is there.

"Many paths dead-end because they only go so far. They can only go as far, as the teacher goes. If you find a teacher who can go forever, then the path goes forever. This is because the teacher is walking ahead into the unknown. If teachers take their students as far as their teachers took them, they are on a dead-end path.

"The Path of Soul does not dead-end. However, few have the courage, the bold, adventuresome spirit to pursue it. Who knows what the limit is on 'as far as you can go'. You can go and go and go and go! I've never found any end to it. I have never seen even the beginnings of an end.

"Now this is not to say I didn't have periods of shaking in my shoes about going further. I use past tense here. Sometimes I have come up upon a darkness that is so dark, that even the light of the darkness is so dark that I tremble as I walk, but I never stop walking. You see, the waters are uncharted. To my knowledge, they have never been mapped out or written down; never because it is very difficult to find adequate words to write it down. Where it stops nobody knows."

Gazelle: "Is the Path of Soul then infinite or is it just a matter of how far each of us can go on the path?"

"The Path of Soul is infinite. I encourage you not to cut yourself short, because it is your birthright to live as Soul. It is your birthright to go as far as you can. And what do you have to lose? You have everything to gain. Why let fear conquer you? If you succumb to fear, you are going to die inside and still you are going to be ruled by that fear. You will then take it with you, into your next life. You will wake up in a dream world without a body, living that same fear and then be sucked back into a physical life, living that same fear again. What's the point? You will continue to come back into this life until you achieve a consciousness free of fear, as one who can walk the infinite path."

Gazelle: "Is fear then, just a fear of waking up and walking the path?"

"It is a fear of the unknown. Like I said, I tremble sometimes, but my trembling is not a mental trembling. It is an actual trembling caused by the vibration of the unknown itself. I'm not saying that here in physical life you would see me tremble. My body is stable, but I am aware of the trembling that occurs on another level.

227

"Along with that trembling comes a new power, which one does not experience until they begin to live it. Suddenly the energy rolls through your body in such a way that you can deal with the trembling and you can move on. So, when you are given one thing, you are given the energy to deal with it, and that energy can be called upon in an instant. You simply put your attention on it and it is there. It is a very real, moving energy with a strong flow to it that suddenly just consumes your being. You are not left in the lurch while you are walking into the unknown.

"So, there is really nothing to be afraid of. At the point in the dreamtime, when you fully recognize the dream that you are living and have the recognition of the God-self existing within you, you then naturally have the nerve to go forward. It's not really courage, it goes beyond courage. The nerve to go forward suddenly becomes born in you. When this state occurs, then you will go through the eye of the needle and experience omnipresence. At this point, the mind no longer controls anything, because the mind no longer says, 'This is how you do this. This is how you do that.' You simply do it!

"There is nothing to be afraid of on the Path of Soul because you transcend the mind. You lose your mind, so to speak. And, it goes in varying degrees as you walk the path. This does not mean that you lose your intelligence. It simply means that your mental machinery no longer controls the life force that you carry within yourself."

Gazelle: "It seems I go two steps forward then my mind all of a sudden says, 'Oh No! You're not going to shut me off.' All of a sudden the mental opposition becomes stronger and that is when my fear begins to surface."

"There will come a time when you will be consumed with attention to where you are going and you just won't care any longer. When the mind talks, you just won't pay any attention to it."

Gazelle: "That is what happens! When I don't pay any attention to it, it goes away."

"The brain is a machine, which pumps out information on impulse. Something pushes a button and the mind chatters. Let it chatter. If you don't pay any attention to it, the button itself becomes more relaxed. It will still give you information when you need it, but, at your request, not on automatic pilot. As it is now, the mind is running the show and it jumps in at the darnest times, but it will lose its control."

Two Eagles: "Is your teacher Alana continuing to walk the path, even after her death?"

"When someone attains freedom from the mind to walk the infinite path; when one is no longer controlled mentally and enters or steps into what we call 'The Shaman Consciousness', they have left the fear behind. At that point, there is no stopping that individual on the path. There is nothing that will trip them up at that point. There is no fear. Fear would be the only thing that would stop that person, that consciousness from moving forward!

"If a person achieves Shaman Consciousness and decides at that point to leave the body, that is, to no longer use a physical form, that person becomes ONE with the Void but does not stop expanding within it. The Void is always expanding. The Void is not static. The Void IS and the Void is BECOMING. The Void is Becoming as you and I are Becoming! As individuals come into, not an intellectual recognition of God within themselves but an actual knowingness of living as God, of being as God, of expressing God, then something happens. That person then lives in consciousness as that. God Itself and Void Itself forever expanding.

"So, you see, I guess we could call this 'God's Vanity', but not vanity as you and I know vanity. It is an expression of the energy of God Itself, an expression of the Void recognizing Itself and It is ever-becoming. It is an expression first here in the physical world where it gains recognition of Itself and then It is an expression in all of the other planes, because all the other planes are here and now. There really isn't any separation. When we speak of inward and outward, there is no inward and outward, there is only expression. Do you see? No inward. No outward. *Just being.*"

*Two Eagles: "Will there come a time when the physical world is no longer needed?"*

"No. And the reason I say no is, the Void is infinite, and so there will always be recognition of Itself. So you see, physical life is a privilege. Now, it is a curse if fear stops you, but it's a privilege because, if you take it for what it is, you go for the pot of gold, and beyond. Do you see? Beyond the rainbow.

"It is a privilege to live. The body itself evolves, changes, so it will eventually not be as we know it now, just like it's not the same as it was a million years ago. As the consciousness becomes refined, the body becomes refined.

"There are other people on other planets who have a more refined body. Now we are not saying that everybody on every other planet is above and beyond what is on this planet. That is not true at all. Don't go looking for flying saucers to give your power away to some alien being. Appreciate the body that you are carrying now. This is your energy field, that which you are using to walk the Path of Soul. Treat it well. Keep it healthy. It is worth the trouble of swallowing those vitamin pills. Keep it clean. Attend to its needs. Don't put junk into it. I realize that junk is relative, relative to the refinement that you carry. You get more picky, but picky doesn't mean austere. If a person is living austerely, they are living in fear, aren't they? 'I must live this way because...' And that is fear in itself. Another block.

"You do not give up anything on this path, except the 'little self', which isn't any great big deal. Once you get a handle on that, it is nothing!"

*"When someone attains the freedom from the mind to walk the infinite path, when one is no longer controlled mentally and enters or steps into what we call 'The Shaman Consciousness', they have left the fear behind."*

# THE OLD MAN

**Winged Wolf:** "There was an old beggar man who every day passed by this same person, and this same person never put any coins or folding money into his hands when he begged. He stood there hungry, day in and day out. I suppose other people put money into his hand here and there, but mostly, he was ignored. Everyday this man passed him and he sometimes started to reach into his pocket to give him something, then he just walked away, before he actually got his hands deep enough into his pocket. Maybe those were the days when he looked at the old man and saw the hunger and felt a little guilty so he tried to reach in but no money came out. He never gave anything to the old man. Who knows how many days passed. It could have been years.

"Well, one day he stopped and he gave the old man all the folding bills that he had in his pocket. He took the old man to a soup kitchen and fed him. When the old man finished one bowl of soup, he handed him another. He suddenly felt really good for feeding this old man. The old man, in his gratitude, died. The old man, in his gratitude, <u>could</u> die. To die hungry is to be born hungry. To die without love is to be born without love. The old man may or may not have known; but, somehow or another, he could not die hungry. He lived the same day of his life, hungry, over, and over, and over again, and finally, somebody fed him and he was grateful. He had gratitude in his heart for receiving. That gratitude released him from his hunger and from ever having to be hungry again. And so the old man could die and begin a new life, a new day, and a new cycle.

"The cycles of life that we live are something to be mindful of. To understand where you stand every moment of every day is important but not important. What is important is that you live your life impeccably. You give with an open heart and you receive with an open heart, because receiving is the same as giving. If you can receive, you are able to give. If you cannot receive, you cannot give, or you give with strings attached.

"The old man had been standing on that same corner day after day after day. He could not receive because he had nothing to give. Finally, he was given a gift by someone else who had nothing to give but the money in his pocket, because this younger man was down to nothing spiritually. This younger man was totally bankrupt, spiritually. Because his money had no meaning to him and he saw that it had such meaning to the other man, he said 'the heck with it' and gave it all to the beggar man. And, when he did, he was able to give, and the old man was able to receive and then give with gratitude. His gratitude then filled the younger man's life so that the younger man could be nurtured. The younger man could then have a life of greater fulfillment.

"The younger man could go out into the world and develop his life because he had given. Before, he had only received. Again, one who cannot give, cannot really receive. So, the old man was free and the young man could go on with his life. And that is the way life works for us. Isn't that beautiful! That was probably one of the most important parts of the story, because his giving to the old man made it possible for the story to evolve. How subtle it was. How unnoticed.

"How many times have you seen that story? How many times have you seen *Groundhog Day*? Some of you are captivated by the repetition of watching someone evolving out of an experience, but never quite see what really happened.

"This is what occurs in our daily lives. We get hooked up sometimes in the icons, and not the energy

233

behind the icons. It is the energy story that tells the true nature of a story, the energy behind the icons, behind the images through which you portray life. Pay attention to the energy. If you have an urge to do something and do not do it, next time you have the opportunity, do it. See what happens. Give. Learn to live through your perceptions, through the energy that is put out, not merely through the story that portrays the energy.

"The story that portrays the energy can sometimes be deceptive, but the energy is never deceptive. When you begin to live out the energy story in your own lives and become truly conscious of it, then you will no longer be living the same story over and over again. Now, hopefully the apprentices here, as far along as you are, have already interrupted that cycle. I would say that most of you have, and if you have not, you are in the process of doing so. You are very close to it. Isn't that wonderful? Moments of power. The power is being able to perceive the energy and to act from that perception.

"This is what separates the shamanic life from the monastic life. It is a path of action, of DOing, not sitting and meditating or praying. It is a path of awareness and action. It has nothing to do with conjuring or magical things as most people suppose. The reason they think that it is magical is because it is active. The activeness of the shamanic path is very powerful. Just as you saw in the movie *Groundhog Day*, the young man was released from his karma and able to move forward because he could give. The old man was released from his karma because he could also give, and receive. He experienced gratitude.

"Gratitude is that which keeps an individual out of poverty. It is the key ingredient to living on top of the mountain instead of down in the wallows of poverty consciousness. It is very important that people understand the true meaning of the path and the word shamanism. It is very important. It is what breaks the wheel of karma. It is

real freedom. It is a freedom walk. Are there any
questions? Comments?"

*Leaping Deer: "In the last newsletter it said we present the
image of our energy.* She reads from a letter, *'Whatever you touch
in your personal life and in your apprenticeship grows instantly
into the image of your energy.' Would this mean an evolvement
of your energy?*

"Yes, it would. That was a memo that I sent to you. If you
remember, I spoke a year ago about this being the year
(1995) of expansion, expansion because I, as the hub of
the wheel, and you, as the spoke of the wheel, are joined
together. That is our string of energy. Whatever happens at
one end, happens at the other. Not necessarily do all the
spokes feel all the other spokes, but in a way, they do.
There has been a great expansion here with the move to
'Between the Wind'. There were also many difficulties that
had to be overcome, that were overcome, and that will still
have to be overcome. All of that is part of the life energy
as it exists here. Because you are connected to the life
energy that exists here, you also take that type of
expansion out into your own life.
       "The life energy that exists here, that expands, and
is forever expanding, creates or presents difficulties of its
own nature. Do you see? Expansion always has difficulties
of its nature that have to be dealt with, so you will feel
that, just as I feel that, because we are all connected to the
same life energy. In a family, if there is great movement in
one area of the family and you are strongly connected to
that family, then you would feel that, do you see?
       "We are a spiritual family, an ever-growing,
evolving spiritual family. Because it is the shamanic path,
the life energy never stays the same. It is not a monastic
order where things are the same routine, day in and day

235

out. It is an active path that reflects moment to moment in life as you place your attention in various areas.

"Now you have your attention on a new home. Well, you put your attention on that home and things will flow into it, but you have to constantly keep it the way you want it, not the way someone else feels that you should have it.

"If, in your finances, you try to bend to a place that you do not feel comfortable, because someone else directs you in that way, you will get in trouble. Stand back. Be sure there isn't another way of approaching that same situation. Make it easy on yourself. Know what you can and what you cannot do, and if, at first you do not know and then later into the game you do know, fine. Then let that settle in you, make your decision and stand by it. That way, you expand neatly and cleanly.

"Now, every once in a while there is a lot of activity because it is the shamanic path and activity is the name of the game. It is evolvement through activity. It is evolvement through presentation into the environment, living as Soul. So there is much activity sometimes, because the possibilities, as you are moving about in your own environment, are endless. The activity presents itself and very often you move with it. It takes responsibility then to carry it through, doesn't it? It gets very complicated and very big.

"I even have to pull myself back sometimes and say, 'No, this is a wonderful idea, we are going to do it, but it is ahead of time, slow down'.

"Maintain perspective. Do not rush. Do not let people's excitement and eagerness push you. You are the one paying the bill. Let it be comfortable and right for you. This is the path of wisdom. You learn to live the wisdom that you know.

'The more you give to someone, the more capable of love you are. It is really interesting. My teacher, Alana, used to talk to me about this subject all the time. She used to say, 'You have to give to me otherwise you would not appreciate me'. So I used to give to her just as you give to me, and as you give to each other. Each person receiving becomes very endeared to you and you can interact with them more easily, because you have given to them. You have formed a connection from your end.

"Now, in healthy people and in healthy relationships you do not give to get, but it naturally happens when you give, the other person feels free to give back, so it makes a flow. You never do it for manipulation's sake. You never do it to get something. That is a violation of spiritual law. You give out of divine love, whatever that giving is. You know, when my back hurt, Standing Turtle went down and fed the horse one morning. Wolfsong got in there and rubbed my muscles.

(To Wolfsong, Wings of Change, Two Eagles, Sky Wolf, and Leaping Dear)

"You are out there chopping trees, putting up doors, bringing things from the mainland that are needed here, and doing things wholeheartedly. It is that giving, do you see, that makes you a part of this place. Never hold back in giving to your family or your spouse. I am not saying you do not use wisdom with children, because they have to learn other things from that giving, don't they?

"Look how much fun it is when you give wholeheartedly. When you are wholeheartedly giving, it makes you feel alive. It makes you love that person, or situation, or cause, to which you are giving. People become impassioned to save the Earth when they give their energy into saving the Earth. Do you see? Giving is that important. So the young man, as he gave to the old man, then felt his connectedness to the old man, wanting him to live and, in so doing, he made himself alive. Does that answer your question?"

Wolfsong: *"Mentioning these pine trees and seeing the face in the big tree, tells me there is something about that tree that is striking. I was wondering why it opened itself up to me."*

"You were loving it. All things respond to divine love, even beings that are not sentient. We are talking about the greatest power of all, and that is divine love."

## *"To die without love is to be born without love."*

## *"Give with an open heart and you receive with an open heart because receiving is the same as giving."*

# THE ETERNAL DREAMER

**Winged Wolf:** "In The Beginning, there was nothing. Out of that nothingness came a vibration. Out of that great vibration, came something very akin to feeling. The motion stirred nothing, and in the stirring, there was a new type of vibration that presented matter. This new type of vibration that presented matter was akin to the feeling that life is like a dream. It began in wavy images until it filtered down and manifested in form-like substance.

"The Beginning that was nothing, now was something. Perhaps not something as we know it today, but it was something, a primitive image, maybe a streak in the sky, maybe the sky, maybe a color. As this sequence of events progressed, there became species, and planets where these species lived, earth and ground; not just here, but on many planets.

"Beings came into manifestation as insects and other small forms of life, infinitely small forms of life from the Beginning, all from this vibration of the Void. And, the infinitely small vibrations, and manifestations of these vibrations took various forms. They evolved. They not only evolved in form, but in the essence they carried within them from the Void. *That* essence which they carried within them from the Void is the Prana or Life Force, the Chi, the Tao. It has many names.

"That essence from the Void was what formed consciousness. That essence or life force was Soul. It was Soul that made these species evolve from tiny little creatures, to bigger creatures, to more complex creatures, until humankind. Human beings, in their evolvement, had the capacity to realize the dream, to realize that they could effect the dream. Before then, the animals and the insects effected the dream but they did not know they had

239

the capacity to do so. They evolved from a very primitive life to a higher cultural life, effecting the dream.

"What was thought of as effecting the dream, however, was not quite conscious. People knew that they could make things happen within the dream. They could build homes. They could build cities. They could elect governments to take care of those cities. But gradually, they became so wrapped up in that which they dreamed into their environment, which reflected their own evolvement, that they forgot that they were the dreamer themselves.

"They were the dreamers because they carried the essence of the Void within themselves, the essence of Soul. Every once in awhile one human being had the opportunity to wake up in the dream, to see what it was that s/he was doing. Such unique people became aware enough of their actions and aware of the effects of their actions to recognize that the city, the world in which they lived, their communities and their families were inventions of the mind, and not really solid or real.

"Once in a great while someone came up with that awareness, but usually the realization faded and receded, getting lost in the chaos that was already existing. Perhaps such persons were murdered or sacrificed to keep the masses asleep. The people who murdered them were not necessarily conscious of the dream, only fearful. They did not want to lose power, so the mental inventions had to be perpetuated.

"Still, every once in awhile someone would say, 'This is not real', and, if they did not say it too loudly, they could walk through society and be a little bit different. If they spoke up loudly, then they would be put back into a place so they would live silently again. If they did not cooperate, then they would have to be removed, because that is called a disturbance.

"When one wakes up as Soul, one begins to see that *all life is a conscious dream.* I can tell you about the dream that I dream. It is something like the story you heard today, (*The Buddha's Question*). I dreamed, I dreamed you. This is my dream and you are alive in it. It is also your dream and I am alive in your dream. The karmic strings of energy between us makes this situation possible, my dreaming you and your dreaming me. It is our dream together. You see, you and I are both the Eternal Dreamer. We are both that essence from the Void. The flesh that we wear is an evolvement of our Earth, the planet on which we live. It is a consciousness we have formed from awareness.

"As we live as Soul, we recognize the power to dream. The power to dream means that we recognize ourselves as part of the Void. A part of the Void we call Soul is actually the Godhead Itself, a bit and a piece. But, since there is no such thing as a bit and a piece, because you cannot subdivide something that is nothing and yet everything, that places you and me in a situation of being God the Eternal Dreamer, taking form to experience the reality of being *that.* Reality is the Void. It is the power of the Void. It is THE Expression. How you and I express it, is not reality, it is the dream! The reason we have to take responsibility for ourselves on the Path of Soul is because we are responsible for the dream, your dream with me, my dream with you, and your dream with your family, friends, and co-workers, and theirs with you. God cannot be personified and yet, God is personified through you.

"Without strings of energy to connect, there would be no awakening. There would be no understanding of what we are talking about, and you could not move freely with those individuals with whom you work.

"When one is adept at living as Soul, adept meaning most of a person's life is lived in that state, the personality becomes refined and it takes on the Soul quality. It becomes Soul Light. The refinement of the personality takes all those rough edges off and makes it possible to live without chaos. There is still individual expression through the personality, but refinement makes it kind and gentle. It makes free expression possible without harming another individual or any sentient being. It creates harmony within the individual. When a person lives as Soul most of the time, that which they put their attention upon, manifests through the attention.

"The dreamer does not have to dream per se, in the ordinary sense of the word. A simple picture suffices. The attention locks on it and it becomes manifest. It is reflected in the mirror of life. The mirror of life takes on the form that you give it. You dictate what form that mirror of life takes. It is very simple to make changes in your life, if you are living as Soul. Since there is no mental conflict when you are living as Soul, adjustments are easy. Whatever you put your attention on, can be.

"Many people come to the end of their lives and say, "Well, I visualized or dreamed all my life what I wanted, and I never got it'. The reason they never got it is because they visualized in a way that the mind was in control, which caused constant conflict. As soon as they would visualize something, there would be an opposing image that said, 'No, it won't work', or 'You are not worthy of it'. You are worthy and have a right to have anything, to present anything at all in your existence that you want.

"In essence, you are the Godhead, and you do not achieve things by pushing or pulling to get them. When you do that, you have put the mind in control. The mind is nothing but a computer-like machine. It cannot be the master. It can only be a tool. If you let Soul take command and live from the Third Eye, then Soul uses your mind as a tool. Your mind then becomes very sharp, very capable. It becomes much more capable than it could ever possibly be otherwise.

242

"So you see, people who visualize all their lives, daydream all their lives to have something, have negated their desires, as well as bringing a distorted version of them into existence. They have said that they were not worthy to have their dream or it really would not work out because of 'this and so' in their life. This is conflict.

"The only way out of conflict is through Soul Vision. *The only way out of conflict is through Soul Vision.* Soul Vision has been around since the beginning of life. We simply got caught up in mental inventions and forgot. Now you and I are practicing it again.

"To live as Soul is your birthright and my birthright. It dictates the empowerment of an individual. It reminds the individual who he is. You are the Eternal Dreamer. *You are the Eternal Dreamer.* The Eternal Dreamer is not outside of you. It is you, you as Soul. *You, as a spark of God, are the Eternal Dreamer.* When you leave this life you can consciously dream yourself into another life, if you choose to do so.

"If you spend your time being caught up in other people's hopes, wishes and desires for you, rather than living your own life, what do you end up with? You end up trying to be the fulfiller of other people's wishes and desires, not being yourself, not doing what you want. You will never be content or happy this way and you will have no life at all. You will have lost the power to be the Eternal Dreamer. Do not give your power away to anyone.

"Life is a ripe fruit for you right now. You have dreamed lifetime after lifetime after lifetime in order to align your energies to bring you to this moment. Like the story in the *Buddha's Question,* when the Buddha is talking to a group of children about when he was reincarnated as a plum tree beside a beautiful lake, he made a promise to come back in another life to teach others. He evolved through all those life forms to come to an awakened state in a human body. You are on the brink of waking up and realizing who you are. Do not give that up for anything. It is your birthright. You have earned it."

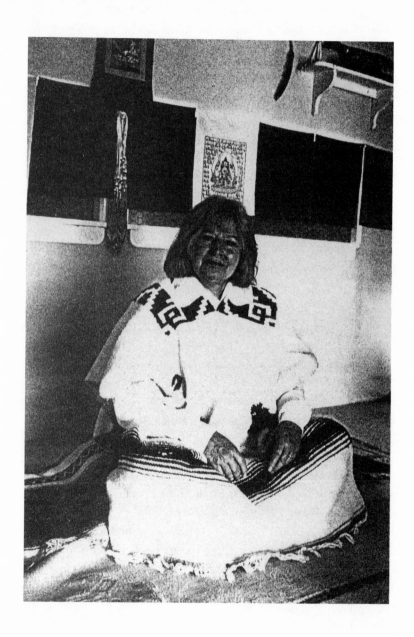

# The Shamanic Path of Soul

You are invited to become an Explorer on
The Shamanic Path of Soul™

It is Winged Wolf's mission to bring the teachings of
The Shamanic Path of Soul to as many people as
possible.

As an Explorer, you shall receive newsletters, and
invitations to attend special functions - Gatherings,
and Assemblys.

There is a $25 annual fee to become an Explorer.
(Please see order form page).

# GLOSSARY

The definitions given in this glossary are particular to their usage in this book and should not be construed as the single or even most common meaning of a specific term.

**Alana:** Winged Wolf's Lakota Shaman teacher; Also known as Alana Spirit Changer.

**Abundance:** The reward of living in the balance of giving and receiving; service.

**Angel:** One who has learned to live as Soul.

**Apprentice:** One who, by agreement with a teacher, is pursuing the Path of Soul.

**Astral:** The plane of duality where manifestation immediately follows a feeling thought.

**Balance:** The freedom from attachment to outcomes.

**Between The Wind:** The name of Winged Wolf's property.

**Black Magic:** To approach someone with ill intent or with the intent to manipulate or to control.

**Chakra:** Sanskrit, meaning 'wheel' or 'disk'; term for the centers of subtle or refined energy in the human energy body.

**Chaos:** A fantasy about what you are doing; an out of control vibration.

**Clarity:** The perspective of seeing life with a quiet mind.

**Companion Energy:** Being so in tune with another, that you resonate together; total acceptance of what is, without opinion or judgment.

**Consciousness:** One's level of awareness of life's dream.

**Divine Love:** Soul's feeling mechanism; producer of joy, compassion and sensor of freedom; accepting life as it is without requiring conditions.

**Dream:** All life as we know it.

**Eagle Tribe:** A society for Shamanic study and exploration under the auspices of Winged Wolf.

**Elder:** One who has passed their first 100 miles in their apprenticeship with Winged Wolf.

**Emotion:** A regurgitated memory with a feeling not originating in the present moment.

**Empowerment:** The power that develops as one's myth is exposed, leaving them natural and authentic.

**Energy:** Soul, life force, the movement of atoms and molecules as enlivened by the breath of the Void.

**Fantasy:** A myth made up by the mind; an awareness manufactured by the imagination to depart from an unwanted situation; visualization.

> "Shamanism means to live in ecstasy, however sometimes we must rearrange ourselves to live there."
> Alana Spirit Changer

**Feeling:** A sensation in the present moment.

**Gathering:** The coming together of Winged Wolf's apprentices and Eagle Tribe members to experience Samadhi.

**God/Void:** Reality, the original energy from which Soul and all life has evolved.

**Gyuto Monks:** An order of Tibetan monks that HU from the base chakra on up to the higher chakras as a necessity for maintaining higher consciousness.

**Happy House:** A learning room where many of the dialogues with Winged Wolf and apprentices occur; also a HUing room.

**Holy:** Natural, authentic.

**HU:** The original vibration or sound of the Void.

**Impeccability:** When intent and action are one; wholeheartedness, living 100 percent in the present moment.

**Journey:** A lesson to be lived and experienced, assigned to apprentices by Winged Wolf to further their progress on the Path of Soul.

**Joy:** The natural result of living as Soul.

**Karma:** A natural result of an action; a reaction to the stillness; the result of the movement of a cycle.

**Kundalini:** Sanskrit, meaning 'snake'; energy force in every being coiled at the base of the spine.

**Little Self:** The expression of being that reflects the myth, ego and/or personality.

**Looking:** A method of 'seeing' without mental comment.

**Manipulation:** Intentional interference with the natural flow or what is; any attempt to control an outcome. A Shaman never manipulates.

**May the Blessings Be:** Let the floodgates be open; Let all things be as they are. All Is, as it should be with no judgment.

**Mental Entrapment:** A state of being caught up in one's mind chatter.

**Milarepa:** Great Tibetan saint and poet 1040 - 1143 A.D.; Refer to *Shaman of Tibet* by Winged Wolf.

**Mind Chatter:** Internal conversations within one's mind.

**Miracle:** A changed consciousness.

**Omnipresent:** Shaman Consciousness; the ability to be everywhere via strings of energy.

**One:** The Void, Soul; we are all ONE as Soul.

**Oozing:** An overspilling of energy.

**Paradoxical Worlds:** Worlds of duality.

**Parallax:** A mystery or riddle to solve which can shift one's perspective on something to present a new opportunity that was previously unavailable.

**Path of Soul:** Living as Soul.

**Present Moment:** NOW.


"Shamanism means to live in ecstasy, however sometimes we must rearrange ourselves to live there."
Alana Spirit Changer

**Quiet Mind:** Living as Soul, Living in a relaxed state of consciousness that is uninterrupted by mind chatter; maintaining inner silence without will power or mind control; operating from direct perception.

**Reality:** The Void, Soul; living wholeheartedly in the present moment.

**Resonance:** Blending to be ONE with what is, companion energy, Oneness with the Void.

**Sage:** An apprentice who has reached a quality or place of refinement, who has been asked by Winged Wolf to guard the Path of Soul and to keep the teachings pure, and has accepted that invitation.

**Samadhi:** A state of consciousness that lies beyond waking, dreaming and sleep; nondualistic state of consciousness; silence.

**Shaman Consciousness:** Living as ONE with the Void, living as Soul; omnipresent.

**Shamanism:** The Path that teaches one to live as Soul in harmony with all life, wholeheartedly in the present moment.

**Shanunpa:** The experience of imitation as a communication, which leads to living in harmony with all life.

**Soul:** The Void made manifest.

**Soul Vision:** Achieved by placing the attention on the Third Eye/Tisra Til; living as Soul evolves out of the practice of Soul Vision.

**Spirit:** The energy of Soul, the Void. (Also the name of Winged Wolf's horse).

**Spiritual Warrior:** One who walks the Path of Soul.

**Stalking:** Imitation of movement to become one with that which is being stalked; useful in the practice of Shanunpa.

**Third Eye:** Also called Tisra Til; the area above the eyes in the center of the forehead; the pituitary gland known as the eye or seat of Soul.

**Thunderbeing:** An advanced apprentice; Having the power of attention, the power of divine love, and power of compassion.

**Translate:** The separation of Soul from the physical body, commonly referred to as 'death'.

**Unconditional Love:** Compassion, the blissful state that results when one recognizes all life as Soul; total acceptance of what is.

**Vision Quest:** Purification of body and mind to be receptive for a shift in viewpoint that will illuminate and clarify.

**Void:** Reality, the original energy from which Soul and all life has evolved.

**White Magic:** To approach something with manipulation and control, with intent to better a position in life.

**Wholeheartedness:** Living 100 percent in the present moment; intent and action are one.

"Shamanism means to live in ecstasy, however sometimes we must rearrange ourselves to live there."
Alana Spirit Changer

# Books

# ORDER FORM:

## Please send me the following by Winged Wolf:

| Quantity | Book Title or Item | Price | Amount |
|---|---|---|---|
| | **BOOKS** | | |
| ____ | Dialogues with a Shaman Teacher ........... | $14.95 | ____ |
| ____ | The Shamanic Journey of Living As Soul... | 10.00 | ____ |
| ____ | Circle of Power ........................................ | 10.00 | ____ |
| ____ | The Flight of Winged Wolf ....................... | 10.00 | ____ |
| ____ | Woman Between the Wind ....................... | 10.00 | ____ |
| ____ | The Shaman of Tibet ............................... | 14.95 | ____ |
| ____ | Doorways Between the Worlds ................ | 10.00 | ____ |

**Also Available at Your Bookstore**

## VIDEO TAPE

| | | | |
|---|---|---|---|
| ____ | The Path of Soul, Sedona Eagle Tribe Gathering. | 19.95 | ____ |

## AUDIO TAPES

| | | | |
|---|---|---|---|
| ____ | Living as Soul .......................................... | 9.95 | ____ |
| ____ | Power of the Spoken Word/Consciousness | 9.95 | ____ |
| ____ | Healing Mother Earth ............................. | 9.95 | ____ |
| ____ | Old Man / Message From Soul ................ | 9.95 | ____ |
| ____ | Parallel Worlds Part 1 / Creation ............. | 9.95 | ____ |
| ____ | Parallel Worlds Part 2 / Memory .............. | 9.95 | ____ |
| ____ | Karma / HU: Song of the Void ................... | 9.95 | ____ |
| ____ | Resolving Karma / HU: Love Song of Void... | 9.95 | ____ |
| ____ | Opening of the Wisdom Eye ...................... | 9.95 | ____ |
| ____ | Light & Darkness / HU: Song of the Void .... | 9.95 | ____ |
| ____ | The Hat and the Fantasy ............................ | 9.95 | ____ |

_____ Beyond Dualities / Healing Powers of Soul.. 9.95 _____

_____ The Eternal Dreamer / Lover & The Beloved 9.95 _____

_____ Stainless Sky / Responsibility ........................ 9.95 _____

_____ Making Yourself Heard / Spontaneity .......... 9.95 _____

_____ Getting Mixed up in Other People's Stuff..... 9.95 _____

_____ Dreaming Voices in the Night / Working in

        Companion Energy.......................... 9.95 _____

SHIPPING: $3.00 one item, $1.00 each additional item. _____

_____ **I WANT TO BECOME A MEMBER OF THE SHAMANIC PATH OF SOUL™ ENCLOSED IS MY ANNUAL MEMBERSHIP FEE OF $25.00**

_____ **PLEASE SEND ME AN APPLICATION FOR APPRENTICESHIP**

                                 TOTAL (USA funds only) _____

# PHONE ORDER: 800-336-6015

_MAIL ORDER - PLEASE PRINT:_

NAME: _____ PHONE: ( ) _____

ADDRESS: _____

CITY, STATE, ZIP: _____

VISA/MASTERCARD No.: _____

EXPIR. DATE: _____ SIGNATURE: _____

Higher Consciousness Books   P.O. Box 268  Deer Harbor, WA 98243

Higher Consciousness Books
P.O. Box 268
Deer Harbor, WA 98243

Higher Consciousness Books
P.O. Box 268
Deer Harbor, WA 98243

If you wish to receive a copy of the latest catalog/newsletter and be placed on our mailing list, please send us this card.

*Please Print*

Name: _____

Address: _____

City & State: _____

Zip: _____    Country: _____

If you wish to receive a copy of the latest catalog/newsletter and be placed on our mailing list, please send us this card.

*Please Print*

Name: _____

Address: _____

City & State: _____

Zip: _____    Country: _____